Intimate
SECRETS

Intimate
SECRETS

Which to Keep and Which to Tell

By KAREN BLAKER, PH.D.

LITTLE, BROWN AND COMPANY

BOSTON   TORONTO

FIRST EDITION

*All of the names in this book have been changed, for reasons of
privacy.*

Library of Congress Cataloging-in-Publication Data

Blaker, Karen.
  Intimate secrets.
  1. Secrecy—Psychological aspects.   2. Interpersonal
relations.   I. Title.
BF637.P74B58   1986   158   86-10623
ISBN 0-316-09948-1

*Material from "Ask Dr. Blaker" program is used courtesy of
WOR Radio, New York, New York.*

RRD VA

DESIGNED BY JEANNE F. ABBOUD

*Published simultaneously in Canada
by Little, Brown & Company (Canada) Limited*

PRINTED IN THE UNITED STATES OF AMERICA

This book is dedicated
to those who know my secrets:

_S_

BOB
SCOTT AND KIM
GRETCHEN AND HARLAN

*"Too much or too little
self-disclosure betokens
disturbances in self and
interpersonal relationships...."*
SIDNEY M. JOURARD,
The Transparent Self

Acknowledgments

Most sincere thanks and gratitude to WOR-AM radio for the opportunity to speak with so many people about secrets through such a wonderful medium; to Sister Loretta Palamara, M.S.C., of the Cabrini Hospice in New York City for her insight into the dying process; to Carole Monroe for her initial work on the project; to my editor at Little, Brown, Ray Roberts, for his support and encouragement; and especially to Janice Rotchstein for her tenacity, her skill with words, and her belief in my idea.

A Secret Journey: The Beginning

I T was 1:05 P.M. on a cold, wintry Tuesday afternoon in a metropolitan radio studio. I put on my headset, adjusted the microphone, and awaited a cue. When the "On Air" sign turned red, I was live in the homes of those who tuned in to hear my call-in advice program. The topic that day was secrets.

I gave out my telephone number and invited the listeners to pick up their phones and talk to me about things they had never been able to tell another living soul.

The lights on the control panel began to blink. I pressed one of the flashing buttons and welcomed the first caller to "Ask Dr. Blaker."

Within seconds I heard a low, tense voice say, "I've never told this to anyone."

After a moment's hesitation, he continued. "It's this habit I've had ever since I was a kid. I'm so embarrassed by it. That's why I couldn't even tell my therapist and I saw him twice a week for seven years."

The man paused nervously and then broke his own silence. "Nobody would believe I could do this. They'd think I was crazy. You see, I'm fifty-eight years old and a vice president of a Fortune 500 Company."

His comments stopped abruptly, and I recognized from years of speaking with people on the air about their psychological problems that this was a crucial time for him. He had begun to weigh the pros and cons of speaking further. Like so many who hear my daily program, he had chosen the anonymity it affords to deal with a personal crisis. But even in anonymity, he seemed frightened to reveal this long-kept secret.

"You sound like you want to talk about this," I said, supporting his desire to continue, and feeling he was fighting with a deeply rooted fear that he would be destroyed if anyone knew what he was concealing.

With enormous effort and a rush of words, he blurted out, "I've always sucked my thumb before I go to sleep."

It was as if the line had gone dead. Only I could hear his shallow breathing and sense his impulse to slam down the receiver. I said nothing, played with the second, and risked his hanging up. I wanted the full impact of what he had said as well as done, which was to tell his secret, to fill his consciousness.

Moments later I asked, "Does thumb-sucking help you relax?"

From his reaction, I knew he hadn't expected this kind of response. Laughter perhaps, a reprimand maybe, or a disconnect in disgust, but not a question that put his nightly ritual in perspective and encouraged him to look at his need for being so secretive.

"Yes, sucking my thumb does relax me," he replied in a surprised tone.

When we began to discuss how other people relieved tension he remarked, "I've never smoked and I've always drunk in moderation. I'm very proud of that." The revelation calmed him and he started to see his behavior as less threatening. "Compared to other habits," he reasoned, "thumb-sucking isn't that awful. Come to think of it, now that I'm not as ashamed maybe I won't do it as much."

I agreed with him. Since he no longer felt so mortified about his habit, he would be less anxious at night and more able to fall asleep without sucking his thumb.

Then he hung up before I could ask him if he was secretive by nature. Often people who have one secret have many others. They find it difficult to discuss with anyone what they have hidden. This type of closed behavior can lead to serious problems.

Whenever you isolate yourself with a secret, you are in danger of falling victim to powerful nonverbal logic. You think to yourself: "I am hiding something about me. I wouldn't hide it unless it was bad. Therefore, I must be bad." Of course, this reasoning is inaccurate but you don't realize that, because you haven't talked about it to see how others will react. Eventually, this train of thought undermines your self-image and makes you feel negative about yourself. If you allow the silent thinking to go on indefinitely, you can begin to experience a wide range of emotional problems, from free-floating anxiety to severe depression.

By allowing his secret to grow and fester in the darkness, the businessman gave it the power to weaken his self-confidence. If he had talked about his thumb-sucking with a close friend, spouse, clergyman or therapist he would not have blown his habit out of proportion or suffered such undue stress.

As I finished discussing my reactions to the corporate executive's problem, I received another call. A woman came on the line and said, "I never have trouble sharing secrets. I can't keep anything from anybody."

I listened as Marge, a sixty-four-year-old widow who lived alone, told me that her dilemma had nothing to do with handling secrets. She phoned because she wanted to know why she didn't have any friends.

I sensed that her dilemma had everything to do with handling secrets except that her problem was the opposite of the corporate executive's. Whereas he had difficulty with secrecy because he kept secrets, she had trouble with disclosure because she told too many. To follow through with my assumption, I asked Marge if she tended to be very open with people from the moment she met them.

"Oh yes," she answered. "Last week, for example, I invited my new neighbor to dinner. She was shy, so I began talking right away. I told her about my own adoption, my homosexual son's illness, and my most recent love affair. She listened, but she wouldn't tell me anything about herself.

"I saw her a few days ago in the hall and she didn't act very friendly. I asked her to tea, but she never showed up."

Marge's voice filled with hurt and she asked, "What am I doing wrong?"

"Perhaps you are telling too many of your secrets too soon," I replied. "It sounds like you are scaring people away."

I then talked with Marge about the dinner she had given and how she had revealed a series of intimate stories. Her guest had probably been shocked and confused. Since she didn't know Marge at all, she didn't feel comfortable enough to respond in kind. She was also no doubt threatened by Marge's open nature and wondered whether *her* confessions would be safe with Marge.

Finally, Marge said that she understood more about why she lost friends. I suggested that she slow herself down when it came to disclosing private information. I encouraged her to engage in more small talk during the first several encounters with a new acquaintance.

After I said good-bye, I switched to a commercial and began thinking about Marge's open nature. Many people find it almost impossible to keep anything to themselves. Their nonverbal logic is: "I would hide something only if it was bad. I don't want you to think I am bad. Therefore, I will tell you all my secrets." This reasoning is dangerous because it motivates people to open up in an indiscriminate way without building trust first. The behavior makes others anxious and they tend to shut you out of their lives. They don't want to hear yet another one of your secret-monologues.

Open behavior can also lead to serious mental health problems such as isolation, confusion, lack of control and depression.

SELF-IDENTIFICATION

Do you identify with the corporate vice president or with Marge? Have you ever found that your approach to secrecy or disclosure has caused problems?

If you are like most people you have some difficulties handling secrets. Your behavior directly influences your emotional well-being and your relationships.

For example, if you tend to have trouble sharing secrets with your spouse or lover, you have a closed nature. This probably makes you feel uneasy about revealing intimate details to others. You do have a right to privacy but when concealment becomes the norm, you can suffer upsetting side effects. Are you experiencing any of them?

- Do you have cycles of general discontent without knowing why?

- Do you have periods of free-floating anxiety?
- Do you have repetitive dreams that you don't understand or dreams that you can't quite remember?
- Do you find yourself frustrated or angry but discover you are unable to tie the feeling to any particular cause?
- Do you fly off the handle for no apparent reason?
- Do you think you are less trusting than you used to be?
- Do you feel distant from a person or group of people with whom you were once close?

Answering "yes" to one or more of these questions could mean that your closed personality and a secret that you are carrying alone could be affecting you in a negative way.

If you tend to disclose secrets impulsively to anyone you meet, you have an extremely open nature. You are likely to find it difficult to withhold personal information. You may even tell other people's secrets that have confidentially been entrusted to you. Although you may regret your actions later, you don't seem able to modify your behavior.

It is important to be open with others about yourself to gain their support and to increase the intimacy you share. Unfortunately, when secret-spilling is the norm, there are major repercussions. Are you feeling any of them now?

- Do you have fears that someone will misuse the information they have about you?
- Do you often feel rejected because people don't reciprocate with the same level of intimate stories that you are sharing?
- Do people hesitate to trust you with truly sensitive information?
- Do you feel angry or frustrated when you conceal anything from others?
- Do you find yourself confused when you are with people because you don't know what you have told them?
- Do you feel anxious with silences or small talk and so fill in the gaps with revelations that you later regret disclosing?

Responding "yes" to one or more of these questions could indicate that your open personality and secret-spilling could be causing you problems.

The Power of Secrecy/Disclosure

Are you surprised that the way you deal with secrets can have a potent effect on your life? You are not alone. Most people have no idea what a powerful force their too open or too closed nature can be.

My initial awareness of the importance of this behavioral phenomenon came while I was in graduate school. My doctoral thesis examined the influence of secrecy and disclosure on couples who were becoming parents for the first time. I found that husbands and wives who did know when to reveal confidences and when to keep them from each other negotiated with ease the role change from being spouse to that of spouse *and* parent. I also discovered that after the birth of the first child, couples who had been closed with one another about their needs, desires, and dreams experienced a higher level of postpartum distress.

Instinctive vs. Learned Response

The ability to use secrets appropriately is not innate. It is something that we all need to learn. I was no exception. Let me tell you a personal story.

Twenty years ago, a married graduate student with a new baby, I took two blouses from a large department store in Los Angeles. I was caught and charged with shoplifting. It was the first illegal thing I had ever done. I was devastated.

I told my father, but the two of us conspired to keep this "terrible deed" from my mother. It was a split-second decision and one that I regretted from the moment it was made. To this day, Father and I tell ourselves that we kept this secret so Mother would not get upset.

As I continued to hide the incident, it began to affect my relationship with my mother. I started to feel distant from her. My father also felt a little alienated because he, too, was holding something back. Still, we both remained in a secrecy pact.

Years later, while I was giving a seminar, I encouraged the participants to think about secret-keeping and secret-telling in their past behavior. As a point of departure, I began talking about the shoplifting episode. It was the first time I had discussed it with anyone since 1965. I brought the incident up because I thought it was in the past. I was wrong.

Disclosing my experience before the class, I started to realize that my having been closed about the shoplifting episode was continuing to create problems in my life. I was still anxious about making the incident known, guilty about keeping it from my mother, and concerned about involving my father in a secrecy pact.

Following the class, I made a decision. At the next family reunion, I carried out my plan. I told my mother what had happened. Her reaction was gentle and understanding. She was merely puzzled about why I had felt unable to tell her my predicament at the time when it had occurred. My father was also relieved that he no longer had to keep a secret from the woman he loved.

Of course, I felt better. By being revealed, the incident had lost its power to trigger anxiety and guilt.

After that illuminating experience with secrecy abuse I began looking at the way I treated secrets and focusing more on how people in general deal with personally sensitive information. I began considering, through thousands of hours with my private clients as an interpersonal relationship therapist, hundreds of callers asking for advice during my radio program, and thousands of letters that were addressed to my nationally syndicated newspaper column requesting help, why they tend to be open or closed.

Discovering that there was little material on the broad spectrum of interpersonal secrecy/disclosure behavior, I decided to write *Intimate Secrets*. I realized there was a real need for a book that would help people avoid the negative side effects of being either too open or too closed.

OUR JOURNEY BEGINS

To help you take the mystery out of when to conceal and when to reveal, I would like you to travel with me deep into your self and look at how you manage private information. Initially, we will explore the basics of a too open and too closed nature and how you may be entrapped in secret-lockjaw or secret-spilling. Then we will examine your interpersonal secrecy/disclosure universe and who is privy to your innermost thoughts. What we uncover may indicate why you are having trouble in some relationships but not in others. From there, we will move on to pinpoint exactly how open or closed you are and why your secrecy/disclosure pattern may be causing you problems.

Then you and I will travel back in time. We will trace your stages of growth and development from infancy through adolescence and the effect your maturation had on shaping your open or closed nature. Knowing why you became as secretive or as nonsecretive as you did, you will be able to start modifying your behavior.

Once we have studied your past, we can delve into your present and examine the pitfalls of secrecy and disclosure in your adult life: how keeping and telling secrets inappropriately can harm your romantic relationships, family, professional life, and dying moments. After we have identified the dangers, you can learn ways of avoiding them.

Finally, we'll discuss the basic skills you can develop to make your dealings with secrets practically foolproof.

An important part of your journey will be the quizzes that you will take in the book and the many composite case studies of people with intimate secrets that you will read. These materials will give you further insight into your secretive or nonsecretive nature.

At the conclusion of our journey, you will have found the right balance for you with regard to your personal secrecy/disclosure behavior. With irrational secretiveness at one end of the spectrum and compulsive disclosure at the other, you will see that mental health falls somewhere in the middle.

Initiating this probe into your past and present reminds me of a comment by a psychologist and family researcher, Mark A. Karpel, Ph.D. He wrote: "Facing secrets involves personal responsibility for one's own actions and/or holding the other(s) responsible for theirs."

Such confrontations require courage and conviction in the face of fears and doubts about the outcome.

You have the courage, because you have picked up this book. I am convinced you will find just rewards in your search.

For example, you may decide to tell a few carefully selected people some deeply guarded secret. Or you may make a resolution to stop living such a heavily secret-laden life. It is also possible that you will come away from this experience promising yourself that you will keep more secrets and not be so open with everyone.

Contents

PART ONE

The Basics of Secrecy/Disclosure

I

Secrets: Friend or Foe?

Y OU are by yourself or with another person or part of a group. Suddenly you find yourself involved in something that is socially taboo or personally threatening.

Soon you are considering whether or not to hide what you have done or heard. Perhaps you were party to a crime or maybe you realized how much you hate your mother-in-law. Then again, you may have been told about an illicit affair or that your best friend's husband prefers ladies' underwear.

Your decision about whether to keep the event a secret by passively withholding the information or to tell others by an active revelation may be a conscious determination. More frequently, however, you may begin either keeping or telling the information without much thought. You are doing what seems "right."

Think back to a recent unsettling experience. Did you talk about it or are you still keeping it under wraps? How are you feeling about your decision? Was telling it a positive or negative experience? Is covering it up making you feel better or worse about yourself?

You are not alone if you sense you could have handled your secrecy or disclosure decision in a better way. Being able to make the appropriate choice involves understanding a complex set of perceptions, decisions, and behaviors. Most of us are not raised with such knowledge, which is why we tend to be either too open or too closed with personal information.

A TIME FOR CHANGE

Are you tired of being afraid to reveal your innermost thoughts? Do you wish you could keep a secret? Would you like to share confidences without upsetting friends? Do you have one or two big secrets about yourself that have been bothering you? Do you want to open up but don't know how?

If you have answered yes to any of these questions, it is time to change the way you deal with secrets by developing new secrecy/disclosure skills. Once you do, you will be able to judge when in the future it is best to tell secrets and when it is best to keep them to yourself.

By making the appropriate choice you will be able to protect your privacy without feeling guilty and increase your interpersonal intimacy without compromising your vulnerability.

You can start to modify how you treat secrets by understanding the basics of secrecy/disclosure behavior: what its purpose is, how it works for and against you, what happens when it is mishandled, and how your too open or too closed nature can lead to the misuse of secrets.

The Purpose of Secrecy/Disclosure

Secrecy/disclosure plays an integral role in the success of your relationships and the strength of your emotional well-being. It enables you to deepen intimacy, enhance your self-esteem, and guard your privacy.

Through disclosure you can feel closer to others and their response can give you personal insight. With secrecy you can maintain your individuality and protect your relationships.

When your secrecy/disclosure behavior is appropriate, you experience positive rewards. When it is inappropriate because you have been either too open or too closed, the negative side effects can be far-reaching.

WORKING FOR YOU

If you deal with concealed information in a constructive way, you can:

- protect your privacy or that of a loved one or close friend from outside scrutiny,
- feel more in control of your life by deciding who knows what about you,
- develop a sense of self that allows you to feel separate in a healthy way from your friends and family.

Revealing confidences appropriately can also result in many benefits. For example, you can:

- gain perspective on an experience that has been unsettling,
- increase intimacy and strengthen alliances with those you love,
- help others understand their own behavior by sharing a private experience of yours.

When you handle secrets and disclosures properly you will reap the rewards. You will feel protected, trusted, loved, and much less anxious.

WORKING AGAINST YOU

Secrecy/disclosure becomes problematic when you abuse information. By being either too closed or too open, you harm yourself and others.

For example, if you hide information in an inappropriate manner, you can:

- trap yourself and others into perpetuating deviant acts such as incest,
- divide loyalties among friends and loved ones when some are privy to the facts and others are not,
- idealize your own or someone else's behavior so that destructive behavior goes unchecked,
- blackmail a person to do your bidding and find yourself in a web of intrigue.

On the other hand, if you tell too much to the wrong people, you can:

- create problems for someone by exposing that person's fault to outsiders,
- harm your interpersonal relationships because your indiscriminate disclosure labels you as untrustworthy,
- involve yourself in a vengeful act that boomerangs.

When you misuse secrets or disclosures you feel the repercussions. You experience undue stress, lose friends, and experience self-doubt.

Most of us do not set out to mishandle secrecy or disclosure. We would prefer to receive its benefits. Should you, however, find that you have not been enjoying its advantages, you will want to examine how you manage secrets.

The way you conceal and reveal personal information is defined by your secrecy/disclosure nature. You developed this behavioral style while you were growing up. Your family was your primary influence, but you were also affected by how you saw neighbors, teachers, and other adults treat secrets.

I have found that there are three basic secrecy/disclosure natures: the open nature that tends to tell secrets impulsively, the closed nature that tends to keep information irrationally, and the balanced nature that uses secrecy and disclosure appropriately. An open or closed nature can abuse secrets and cause mental health problems, whereas a balanced nature can fulfill the purpose of secrecy/disclosure behavior and stimulate emotional well-being.

There is a range of secrecy/disclosure behavior within each of the three natures. This can be illustrated on a continuum, which indicates how the spectrum of handling secrets reaches from being completely open to completely closed.

SECRECY/DISCLOSURE
CONTINUUM

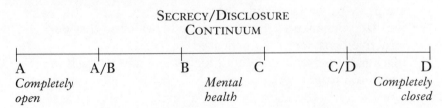

A   A/B   B   C   C/D   D
Completely   Mental   Completely
open   health   closed

If you are too open, you will misuse secrets because you feel uncomfortable about keeping information to yourself. You will fall between points A and B on the continuum. Your general response to dealing with confidential information will be indexed around A, A/B or B. Those points are best described as:

A: You feel compelled to tell all to everyone.
A/B: You feel it is necessary to reveal a lot to acquaintances.
B: You feel slightly pressured to tell more personal information to friends.

If you have a balanced nature, you use secrets in an appropriate way. You will fall between points B and C on the continuum, a range reflecting mental health. You have a skill we can call secret savvy, which enables you to know when and what to conceal and reveal.

If you have a too closed nature, you will misuse secrets because you tend to find revealing confidences a difficult experience. You will fall between points C and D on the continuum. The general way you treat confidences will be indexed around C, C/D, or D. Those indices are best described as:

C: You feel slightly uncomfortable telling personal information to acquaintances.
C/D: You feel uneasy about disclosing private experiences to friends.
D: You feel unwilling to talk about yourself to anyone.

The point where your secrecy/disclosure nature falls on the continuum indicates how you handle secrets and how your emotional well-being is affected by your behavior. As the points on the continuum move away from the center in either direction, the abuse of secrets increases. The farther you are from points B and C, the more likely you are to misuse secrets and to experience mental health problems.

To show you how a person with a too open or too closed nature can abuse a secret and cause a potential mental health crisis, I would

like to introduce you to two women: Alice, usually is open by nature and is at point A/B on the continuum, and Jill, who is closed by
nature and falls at point C/D. Alice usually reveals too much and
Jill never enough.

Both women are about to become involved in an incident that will
be personally threatening and will stimulate a secrecy/disclosure
decision. Although their respective case histories are hypothetical,
they are representative of cases I have handled, and Alice and Jill are
composites of clients I have treated.

Alice and Jill have the same problem: each has an insensitive,
hostile mother-in-law. The two women will deal with the situation
differently because of their different natures. Both women will find
that their behavior will cause negative side effects.

As we follow Alice's and Jill's stories, we will climb the Steps of
Secret Misuse. This ascent will illustrate what people with an open
or closed nature go through before, during and after they make an
inappropriate secrecy/disclosure decision.

THE STEPS OF SECRET MISUSE

```
                                    7. Resolution
                                6. Reevaluation
                            5. Confrontation
                        4. Refuge
                    3. Secrecy/Disclosure Decision
                2. Motivators to Conceal or Reveal
            1. The Incident
```

The first step is taken when you or someone you know experiences an incident that is personally threatening or socially taboo.
The second slips under your foot when you are motivated to either
conceal or reveal what happened. The third comes into play when
you make a secrecy/disclosure decision. The fourth becomes a ref-
uge in which you live with your choice. The fifth makes you realize
your decision was inappropriate. The sixth offers you a chance
to rethink your choice, and the seventh lets you settle the situation.

As you make this climb with Alice and Jill, you will begin to gain
the knowledge that will be essential if you are to modify your too
open or too closed nature.

STEP 1. THE INCIDENT

When something personally threatening happens to you or someone you know, you will begin to have secret reactions to what occurred. If you have a too open or too closed nature, you will have placed your foot on the first step of secret misuse.

It is on that step that we will meet Alice and Jill and start their stories.

ALICE

On her wedding day, Alice was very happy until she saw what her mother-in-law was doing. Whenever she could, the woman found fault with Alice, demeaned her in front of her son, and told stories about her to the guests.

Alice was hurt and angry. She began to hate the woman. She was ashamed of her rage and hatred because a bride is supposed to love her new family.

JILL

On her wedding day, Jill was very happy until she saw what her mother-in-law was doing. Whenever she could, the woman found fault with Jill, demeaned her in front of her son, and told stories about her to the guests.

Jill was hurt and angry. She began to hate the woman. She was ashamed of her rage and hatred because a bride is supposed to love her new family.

Alice and Jill were so unsettled by what had happened at the wedding that they began to have secret reactions to their mothers-in-law.

STEP 2. THE MOTIVATORS TO CONCEAL OR REVEAL

After the incident occurs, there are two motivators that cause you either to keep the experience private or to tell what transpired. Those motivating forces, the protection of your image and the need for control and separation, are influenced by your upbringing which also played an important part in the development of your secrecy/disclosure nature.

Your Image

The way you present yourself to others is probably no accident but rather a carefully staged performance. Most of us grew up molding ourselves into an ideal image. Initially we imitated the best in our parents, and later we combined those attributes with the ones observed in people we particularly admired. During this maturation we were constantly making choices, some more conscious than others, that influenced the way we wished the world to view us. Now we are committed to preserving that image.

Secrecy or disclosure lets us mask the characteristics that do not jell with our calculated persona or to set the record straight if we have been maligned.

Control and Separation

It is natural to want to be in control of ourselves and our lives and also to be separate from others. Secrecy and disclosure play an important role in enabling us to experience these two heady sensations. Controlling information, by either keeping or telling secrets, allows us to keep a rein on the perceptions others have of us and helps us feel like powerful, separate individuals in charge of our lives.

Alice's and Jill's upbringings influenced their too open or too closed natures and affected their images and need for control and separation.

ALICE

Alice was brought up in a family where everybody knew everyone's business. Parents and children alike shared their lives with each other as well as outsiders. Alice and her four sisters lived in a dormitory-type room where there was no such thing as ownership. This lack of privacy and the family's indiscriminate telling of secrets made Alice feel as if she couldn't solve

JILL

Jill was raised by parents who controlled the outside world's perception of the family by refusing to discuss anything personal with outsiders. They encouraged Jill and her brother to be highly secretive. The family's closed nature was destructive. Jill's mother, for example, became very depressed after her son was born, but her husband never encouraged her to her own problems unless she discussed them with others. Growing up with this assumption, Alice concluded that she needed to depend on others for solutions. She had developed little self-reliance.

After the mother-in-law experience, Alice felt that it would be best to protect her image and maintain control by involving others in her problem.

seek help even after two suicide attempts. Seeing this type of behavior, Jill decided she should hide her own imperfections, one of which she felt was her anger.

After the mother-in-law experience, Jill felt that it would be best to protect her image and maintain control by not showing her anger or hatred. If she could appear unbothered by the incident, she could maintain control.

Alice and Jill, each in her own way, had been motivated to consider disclosure and secrecy as means of dealing with her problem.

STEP 3. SECRECY/DISCLOSURE DECISION

If your image and need for control and separation are threatened by an incident, you will want to either conceal or reveal what has happened. You will make your decision in one of two ways. It will be a split-second, impulsive choice, or it will be an unconscious decision that you will realize you made only as time passes and you consistently tell others about the incident or keep it a secret.

Alice's decision was impulsive. Jill's was unconscious and developed over a period of time.

ALICE

On her honeymoon, Alice decided to reveal her mother-in-law's remarks and her own angry reaction to everyone. She even told the front desk clerk what had happened.

Her husband asked Alice to stop discussing the incident with every-

JILL

On her honeymoon, Jill put her mother-in-law's remarks out of her mind. She repressed her rage and hatred. Jill reasoned that newlyweds have better things to do than talk about mother-in-law problems.

one. He added that they were newlyweds and had better things to do
than   talk   about   mother-in-law
problems.

Alice felt that she was at least attempting to solve her problem by
revealing her feelings to everyone and hearing what they had to say.
Jill, on the other hand, never actively decided not to discuss the incident. Even after the honeymoon, it just never seemed as if there
was a good time to bring it up. Only years later did she realize that
it had become a destructive secret.

STEP 4. REFUGE

Once you have concealed or revealed an incident, you start living
with your choice. If you have been too open or too closed, you will
begin to experience disclosure strain or secrecy strain. Either condition stimulates a series of negative side effects that can lead to a
mental health crisis.

Disclosure Strain: Open Nature

If you are an open person you probably discuss your private
thoughts with a lot of people. When you do this in an inappropriate
manner, you experience symptoms of isolation, personal confusion,
and lack of control.

ISOLATION

Your concern that you will not be accepted unless everyone knows
what has happened has spurred you on to tell as many people as
possible about the incident. The result is that loved ones and close
friends have begun to back away from you. They are tired of hearing about the situation and its repercussions in your life. Eventually,
they become uninterested in your plight because you have over-
loaded them with too much secret information.

You begin to feel alone and deserted. You start to miss the intimacy you shared. Instead of looking at how your behavior is chasing
people away, you seek out new people to tell your story to in order

to reduce your anxiety. Soon these acquaintances react as your friends did and you become even more isolated.

PERSONAL CONFUSION

Since you feel you are not able to solve many personal problems on your own, you reveal your private thoughts to others. They respond with divergent points of view. You become confused because you don't know whose advice to follow.

As you continue to tell more people about the situation, you feel as if you are standing on shifting sands. You become frozen as to a course of action. You have lost your self-reliance, and instead of resolving what is bothering you, you let it fester.

LACK OF CONTROL

After a time, you realize that you have discussed the episode with a number of people. Although you know some of them, you recognize that others were just passing acquaintances. You begin to wonder if anybody will use the information against you.

You start to sense that you have lost control over your private thoughts. This causes you to worry about possible repercussions that could hurt you, your family, or friends.

If you continue to be too open, your disclosure-strain symptoms increase. Should the condition go unchecked, you can experience a severe mental health crisis, maybe even a nervous breakdown.

Secrecy Strain: Closed Nature

If you are basically a closed person, you tend to hide information inappropriately. As your secret ages, you become increasingly concerned that you will be found out. This fear causes you to suffer anxiety, blocked emotional growth, and a distancing from others.

ANXIETY

The perceived threat that your secret will be uncovered and will cause you to be rejected makes you feel anxious. Your symptoms may be heart palpitations, trembling, breathlessness, or sweating.

You may attempt to reduce the anxiety by evaluating the pros and cons of opening up. Disclosure would help alleviate the distress, but frequently it is deemed too risky.

Problems compound as you opt for further secretiveness and a way to reduce your stress. The Band-Aid you choose is often some type of self-destructive, compulsive behavior such as overeating, drugs, alcohol, or gambling. Nothing is solved and the dilemma increases.

BLOCKED EMOTIONAL GROWTH

As you continue to carry the secret, your guilt feelings intensify and your fear of discovery escalates. These strong emotions begin to distort your view of the world. They freeze you into a defensive position with other people because you have to be ever alert to protect your privacy.

It is not going too far to say that keeping a major secret places you in a paranoid stance where you perceive others as threatening and yourself as a potential victim.

This distortion stops you from experiencing intimate relationships and blocks you from many opportunities for emotional growth.

DISTANCING FROM OTHERS

Since being intimate and being highly secretive are a contradiction, you find yourself withdrawing from the very people you need.

When you stop asking for help and love, your secret becomes your only companion. As a result, aloneness leads to loneliness and ultimately to depression.

Secrecy strain increases as you continue to isolate yourself with your secret. Eventually these symptoms can lead to a severe mental health crisis. Many cases of nervous breakdowns and suicides have been linked to chronic concealment.

We have looked in depth at the side effects of living with an inappropriate secrecy/disclosure decision. Now let's consider how Alice's and Jill's choices each produced a different kind of strain.

ALICE	JILL
Alice made a problematic decision when she told everyone about her private thoughts. In her husband's mind, she trivialized the sit-	Jill made a problematic decision when she buried her feelings about her mother-in-law. If she had trusted her husband with the in-

uation. If she had discussed the experience only with him, he probably would have helped her resolve the problem.

By telling everyone about her mother-in-law, she fanned the woman's derogatory remarks. The more the elderly woman demeaned Alice, the more Alice talked about it. Soon Alice was asking everyone for advice and had become totally confused as to the best course of action. Her husband and friends began to tire of her private-thought spilling. They started withdrawing. Alice tried new people. They listened, but Alice wondered if any of them would use the information against her.

Alice found herself alone, confused, depressed, out of control, and given to public bouts of crying.

formation, he probably would have helped her resolve the problem.

By not speaking up to anyone, she encouraged her mother-in-law to continue her derogatory remarks. Jill sat on her anger. She began to experience extreme anxiety about having her true feelings uncovered. Jill began to suspect that her mother-in-law was out to harm her and break up the marriage. Jill started backing away from her husband and children because she feared she might one day explode with her secret rage.

Jill found herself depressed, tense, and given to private bouts of crying.

Alice and Jill were suffering severe strain because of their decisions. If their individual symptoms increased, each woman would be facing a potential mental health crisis.

STEP 5. CONFRONTATION

There comes a point in time when you realize that your secrecy or disclosure choice must be modified. An event is usually the catalyst that throws you into secrecy shock or disclosure shock, a condition that first numbs you and then shifts you into action.

The numbing occurs because you are surprised that your decision did not solve the problem. You are also staggered by the realization that you may have to expose your secret or stop spilling your private thoughts.

Alice and Jill went into disclosure shock and secrecy shock, respectively, when their mothers-in-law decided to move in with them.

ALICE	JILL
Alice exploded the day her mother-in-law asked to live with them. Alice voiced her hatred for the woman at a dinner party where her husband's boss was a guest. Alice's husband stood up and yelled at her. He told her to shut up about his mother or get out.	Jill panicked the day her mother-in-law asked to live with them. Jill was furious but was afraid to say anything. Still, Jill sensed that the woman would destroy her home and ruin her marriage.
Alice realized that revealing her hatred and anger had not solved the problem. It was worse than ever now that this horrible woman was going to live with them.	Jill realized that concealing her hatred and rage had not solved the problem. It was worse than ever now that this horrible woman was going to live with them. Maybe she would have to run away.

Alice and Jill were left feeling numb and frustrated. They tried to think about what to do.

STEP 6. REEVALUATION

If you are suffering from secrecy shock or disclosure shock, you will attempt to alleviate the condition by rethinking your original decision.

You may consider resolving your problems by running away, blaming someone else, or lying about the experience. These three courses of action do not solve the dilemma. They only compound the existing difficulties.

The best way to handle a problematic decision is to discuss the situation with an uninvolved, nonjudgmental third party who will honor your confidentiality and give you a perspective on what has happened. You might speak to a close friend, mate, lover, clergyman, or mental health professional. By talking with one of these individuals, you can decide upon the best direction to follow. You can also determine how you can repair the relationships that have been damaged since you made your initial decision.

Alice and Jill sought professional help. Jill went to her minister and Alice to a psychologist.

ALICE	JILL
Alice learned that her hatred for her mother-in-law was triggered by more than the woman's sarcastic remarks. Alice soon realized that she was threatened by the woman's closed nature. She never knew what her mother-in-law was thinking. Everyone in Alice's own family had been so open.	Jill was encouraged to confide in her husband about her long-standing feelings toward her mother-in-law. The minister knew Jill's husband and was sure he would come to her aid if he knew of her distress.
Alice was advised to handle her anxiety by thinking carefully before she spoke about her feelings. She was also advised to work on her mother-in-law's housing problem with her husband. Perhaps he could come up with some alternatives.	The minister reassured Jill that once she revealed her secret to her husband, he would begin to help his mother find an alternative housing arrangement.

Alice and Jill followed the advice that they had been given.

STEP 7. RESOLUTION

Once you have decided how to resolve your inappropriate secrecy/disclosure decision, you are ready to activate your plan. You will either share your secret, so that something can be resolved, or you will stop spilling the secret, so it can be put to rest.

When you have the problem all cleared up, your disclosure-strain or secrecy-strain symptoms will subside.

Alice and Jill found that their solutions ended years of aggravation.

ALICE	JILL
Alice's husband was delighted when she agreed to be more closed about her anger at her mother-in-law.	Jill's husband was hurt that she hadn't trusted him enough to confide in him about his mother's behavior. He encouraged her to be more open in the future.
He was sympathetic about her feelings toward his mother. He admitted that she was a difficult woman.	
Together, they found an apartment for her not far from their home.	Together, he and Jill found an apartment for his mother not far from their home.

After Alice and Jill turned their secrecy/disclosure decisions around, they found that their needs were satisfied, their marital relationships improved, their disclosure-strain and secrecy-strain symptoms were relieved, and their tense interactions with their mothers-in-law ceased to cause them as much difficulty.

ALICE'S AND JILL'S LEGACY

By following Alice's and Jill's stories, you have watched an open and closed nature at work. You have seen how people with both types of personality misuse secrets and suffer negative side effects. You have also discovered how those types of people can seek help to modify their respective natures and solve their individual problems.

I'd like you to think of Alice's and Jill's case histories as your legacy. As Alice and Jill changed, so can you. As they developed secrecy/disclosure skills, so will you.

Now that you know the basics of secrecy/disclosure behavior, it is time to use this information to uncover your approach to handling secrets.

2

Who Knows You Best?

ROTARIAN MAN-OF-THE-YEAR
IS ALSO MURDERER-ROBBER

THE headline spoke of a "Jekyll and Hyde," and of a man with a most extremely secretive way of life.

Tom Milligan was considered a family man, a great Little League coach, a perfect Rotarian, and a responsible businessman.

When he was pulled from the river, a suicide, he left a different past, one littered with robbery and murder, including the fatal beating of his wife, Annette.

The small New York town where Milligan lived was shocked. Even Charlie Lewis, the chief of police, broken in on the streets of Manhattan and Brooklyn, had been duped. Nobody suspected that in the middle of the night, Tom Milligan, dressed in commando clothes and a ski mask, would disappear. Nor did they know that when he returned the next morning he scanned the local television news crime reports and the daily papers for details of his forays.

His sixteen-year-old daughter, Pamela, was the first to expose her father's double life when she told the sheriff how her father had just kidnapped her mother and herself and how she had been released only after her mother had agreed to stay behind. The sheriff refused to believe Pamela, saying that Tom Milligan wasn't that kind of guy. Pamela returned an hour or so later carrying a bag stuffed with handguns and two submachine guns. After she explained that they were her father's, the sheriff and his deputy followed her immediately to where Milligan was holding his wife. When they arrested him, they found in his possession a stolen van laced with stolen plates and a trunk filled with $29,000 in cash.

At police headquarters, Annette Milligan described the midnight disappearances of her husband and his stories about killing three people and robbing a bank. She said that she and Tom had been married for seventeen years and together had been raising three sons and a daughter. Annette admitted that until now, she could never have discussed what else was going on in their home. She feared not only for her life, but for her children's lives.

Annette further recounted how she had somehow gained the courage, several months before, to separate from her husband. In her eyes, although the marriage had ended before it began, she had felt too trapped to leave until then. After spending several hours with the police, she left.

Shortly after he was released on $40,000 bail, Milligan bought a shotgun and went looking for his wife. He found her with twenty-one-year-old Kenneth Anderson and killed them both, shooting Anderson and then beating Annette to death with his gun.

According to authorities, Milligan left the scene, drove to a nearby bridge, and parked his car. He placed his billfold on the front seat, took off his shoes, and jumped. Two months passed before his body was recovered, and the police were called to make a positive identification.

More than a year after the incident, Police Chief Lewis was quoted as saying, "Nothing in Tom's daily routine gave us an inkling he was leading a secret life. I still haven't run into anyone who didn't react with total disbelief. It never dawned on us that Tom Milligan was anything else but what we saw."

This may sound like a scenario for a television movie. It isn't. The story is true. Today, Milligan's younger sons are living with his brother in another town. Of the older children, only Pamela remains in the place filled with the memories and the people who still marvel at what happened.

Tom Milligan may be unusual, but he is not unique. People like him develop two separate individual personalities: one appears to function within society's norms and the other exists in a secret underworld of antisocial or taboo behavior. Compounding this dual nature is the person's need to remain closed to others so that they have no idea what is going on or what to expect next.

SECRETS AND YOUR INTERPERSONAL UNIVERSE

Are you what you appear to be? How much of yourself do you reveal? With whom and how often do you share your secrets?

Answering those questions can help you begin to understand your secrecy/disclosure nature and why it might be causing you problems.

Whether you are aware of it or not, you exist in the center of your own interpersonal universe. Around you orbit the various people in your life — from those who are the closest to those who are the least important. These individuals run the gamut from mate or lover to friends and acquaintances; from parents and business associates to children and siblings.

Within your galaxy you decide how private you want to be by creating a boundary around you that is either more or less permeable. This invisible guardrail lets you control how much information you release while at the same time enabling you to choose who will know you most intimately.

There are basically three different interpersonal secrecy/disclosure universes, and within each there can be degrees of variation. Universe I is aligned with a balanced nature, Universe II with an open nature, and Universe III with a closed nature. Let's look at the galaxies before you decide which describes you best.

Universe I puts the "self" in a boundary that is permeable but not too open nor too closed. This "self" shares most secrets with those in the nearest orbits, as these individuals are known to be trusting and supportive. Occasionally, the "self" will try out a person who is more distant, in an effort to expand his or her close contacts and see if, through reciprocity, additional intimacies can be established. If an even exchange of secrets and mutual feelings of goodwill ensue,

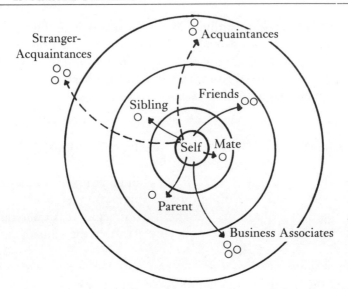

Universe I. A permeable "self" discloses secrets to appropriate people, who will not exploit the information and who will offer insight and support. The diagram shows one example of a Universe I type of person who has a balanced secretive nature.

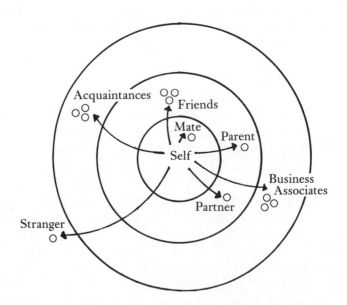

Universe II. A too permeable "self" allows the indiscriminate scattering of secrets, which causes a loss of intimacy with friends and a chance of detrimental exposure with acquaintances. This diagram shows one example of a Universe II type of person, who has a too open nature.

the acquaintance will move into another orbit aligned more closely with the "self" and will become a friend.

This universe allows for the healthy flow of intimacies so that the "self" does not experience isolation, but still maintains its individual boundaries. Universe II has the "self" in a boundary that tends to be too permeable. Secrets are divulged rather indiscriminately. When this occurs, the "self" is usually exposed and vulnerable to people who may misuse the information that has been shared. Sometimes being too open causes those who hear the confidence to back away because they find themselves on "privacy overload" and feel uncomfortable being privy to so many intimate actions and thoughts.

A person who is at the center of this cluster of orbits has a strong need to be understood and loved, but when secrets are used to gain attention and affection, relationship problems arise.

Universe III contains a "self" that is too impermeable. Private matters are carefully screened and, at times, kept even from those who are in the closest orbits. This guarded nature makes the "self" an island and a place for personal secrets to be marooned. In this

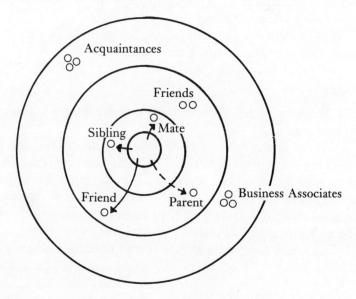

Universe III. A too impermeable "self" has a tendency to prevent the sharing of secrets with others. In the process, it is inclined to create an isolated environment. This diagram represents one example of a Universe III type of person who has a too closed nature.

constellation, the symptoms of prolonged concealment often set in, and, as intimates are locked out, the "self" is left isolated and alone.

An individual living within this galaxy tends to have to some degree a suspicious nature. Trusting others is difficult.

TOM MILLIGAN'S UNIVERSE AND YOURS

It is probably quite obvious that Tom Milligan lived within Universe III. An extreme example of the impermeable "self," even his family knew very little about his life. They had to piece the rest of it together by observing his behavior and dress when he went out at night.

Which one of these three galaxies do you feel most accurately reflects your secretive or nonsecretive self? Perhaps the easiest way to identify the correct one is to think back to a time when you needed help with a personal matter, the more recent the better. Whom did you tell? How many people were brought into your confidence? Were those individuals quite intimate with you or were they people you didn't know very well?

Why not answer those questions by filling in this blank Interpersonal Secrecy/Disclosure Universe?

DIRECTIONS:

1. Put your "self" in the center but don't draw a boundary around it until you finish the diagram.
2. Write down the names of those people in your life who make up your interpersonal world. These may include your spouse, parents, siblings, children, lover, business associates, friends, and different acquaintances. Arrange them in the proper orbits, remembering that the closer they align themselves with your "self" the more intimate they are in your world.
3. Describe the personal matter you needed to discuss:

_____

_____

_____

4. Draw arrows from your "self" to every person with whom you discussed this matter.

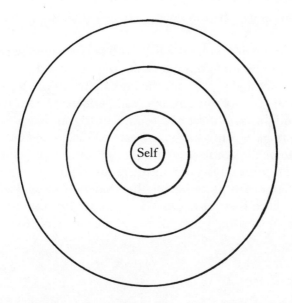

When you finish, look at what you have created and decide which of the three universes you have drawn to illustrate your secret-handling self. Only one of the following statements will be relevant to you:

_____I told appropriate people and perhaps took a risk with a new acquaintance to see if a new friendship could be forged.

_____I tended to be a bit indiscriminate with my personal matter.

_____I shared my confidence with very few people, maybe no one.

Now that you know which universe type you are, sketch a circular boundary around your "self" that indicates how permeable or impermeable your invisible guardrail may be.

WHAT IT MEANS

Identifying the type of universe you tend to reflect shows you how you have been dealing with your secrets up until now. Of course, the content of the confidence has something to do with how freely you revealed the secret. Still, the profile you have drawn should give you insight into your secrecy/disclosure nature and indicate such information as who is most likely to know about your private "self," how many are apt to be privy to such intimate information, and whether you tend to be too open or too closed about your personal life.

If you have had problems with secrets, however periodic they may have been, you may now be able to understand the reasons for the difficulty. Perhaps you told the confidence to the wrong people or maybe you refused to share one with someone supportive. Then again, you might have disclosed too much to too many.

One way to gain control of your secrecy/disclosure behavior is to alter your universe, not necessarily the people in it, but the way you relate to them with your most intimate information.

The first step is to pinpoint just how open or closed you are and why you may be that way. Once you know this about yourself, it will be easier to modify your galaxy to look more like the Universe I model.

3

Here's Looking at You

"I'VE started spanking my wife occasionally and that has really revived our sex life. I'm worried though, do you think we are into S and M?"

The man's voice sounded concerned as he talked to me over the phone during my call-in radio program.

"Tell me why you think it might be sadomasochistic," I replied.

"Well, when I spank her it does hurt her a little. Maybe I should give you some background. My wife and I have been married for twenty-three years and we have had a good sex life but it has never been terrific . . . until lately . . . until I started spanking her.

"About three months ago, my wife, Grace, came home somewhat later than expected. Well, I was relieved to see her because I had been worried. I mean, she is always punctual. So, I got mad at her and said she should have called. I said something like she had been a naughty girl and then, for some reason, added, 'You deserve to be punished.' "

"Go on," I said when he stopped short.

"Well," he began again. "Grace giggled at me and said, 'You're right, Clark, I've been bad. Maybe I should be paddled.' The next thing I know, I'm lifting her skirt, pulling down her panties, and whacking her on the behind.

"Then, Dr. Blaker, I have to tell you, I got turned on. So did

Grace. We made love and it was great. Now, whenever we repeat this naughty-girl game, we find it arousing. I guess the best way to describe it is to say that it gave our sex life some zip.

"But we're worried. We are wondering if we're into S and M — you know, where people beat each other for sexual stimulation."

I quickly asked a few questions. I found that Grace was not being hurt by the ritual, that they were deeply in love, and that the spanking was not being used as a substitute for love and commitment.

"It doesn't sound like sadomasochism to me," I responded. "You have discovered a new way to improve your sex life. Just let me know if things change and either one of you needs more of this kind of stimulation to get excited."

Clark thanked me, adding that he was relieved that their behavior was normal. He said he would stay in touch.

THE SECRECY/DISCLOSURE SCALE

By being open and telling their secret, in this case to a concerned professional, Clark and Grace resolved a dilemma that had begun to provoke undue tension in their lives. If their way of treating this confidence was characteristic of their usual pattern of secret-telling and secret-keeping, they probably have a balanced nature and fall into the center of the Secrecy/Disclosure Scale. This scale is a more specific measure of how permeable or impermeable your "self" is within your Interpersonal Secrecy/Disclosure Universe.

The Secrecy/Disclosure Scale expands upon the Secrecy/Disclosure Continuum of Chapter 1, which reflected the broad range of behavior from openness to complete secretiveness. At the center of the continuum was the balanced nature, synonymous with mental health.

SECRECY/DISCLOSURE
CONTINUUM

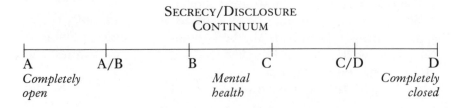

| A | A/B | B | C | C/D | D |
| Completely open | | Mental health | | | Completely closed |

With the Secrecy/Disclosure Scale, you will be able to pinpoint your specific secret-handling nature and exactly how open or closed you tend to be. The scale is composed of seven categories, with the emotional litterbug at one end of the continuum and the closed-off concealer at the opposite end. In the center is the secret savvy pro who mirrors Universe I and a balanced nature. A person who falls in the middle of this scale has a permeable "self," which shares intimacies with appropriate people in the proper place and time. The revelation is done in a positive manner and the results are beneficial. This "self" also knows which secrets to keep.

SECRECY/DISCLOSURE
SCALE

A	A/B	B	C	C/D	D
Emotional litterbug	Gossip gabber	Friendly extrovert	Secret savvy pro	Shy introvert	Guarded withholder	Closed-off concealer

To identify where you fit on the Secrecy/Disclosure Scale, I would like you to take two quizzes. The first is the Case History Quiz, which will help you focus on the type of person you feel reflects the way you deal with confidential information. The second is the Secrecy/Disclosure Scale Quiz; it will position you on the continuum. Both quizzes will categorize you by the way you manage your secrets as well as those of other people. You may find that you are more open or closed with your friends', loved ones', or acquaintances' confidences than you are with your own.

The Case History Quiz

Although each of us is unique, we do have general characteristics that tend to align us with certain groups. Your secretive or nonsecretive behavior may have a signature all its own, even though it is not unlike that of others.

To understand your nature better, take a pencil and read through the following case histories. Check the appropriate space when you find an individual who approaches secrets as you do. His or her story will give you insight into your permeable or impermeable "self," and may even remind you of an incident where keeping or telling a personal story was a problem.

THE EMOTIONAL LITTERBUG

As a high school junior, Mandy had few friends except Anna, whom she had known since the fifth grade. Anna was not a popular girl and for that reason tolerated Mandy's "no-secret-is-sacred" behavior. She realized that her friend used both her own and other people's confidences as a wedge to get into cliques. She also saw how Mandy rarely remained in any of these groups for long. They dropped her once they tired of hearing all her secrets and discovered how she shared their confidences with others. Mandy admitted she had a problem but rationalized that she just kept forgetting her promise to be more discriminatory.

One summer, while Anna was working at a fast-food restaurant, she heard that another girl was getting credit for the nightly cleanup that she, Anna, was doing. Anna complained to Mandy, and within a few days everyone knew that Anna had felt slighted. They criticized her for not handling the situation like an adult by speaking up.

Anna was furious with Mandy for betraying her and refused to accept the excuse that Mandy was only trying to help. Anna cried that she had been burned for the last time and broke off the friendship.

Anna still saw Mandy around school, but they never spoke. One thing remained the same, however; Mandy was either by herself or with someone who had yet to learn of her secret-sieve nature.

Emotional litterbugs like Mandy have not matured enough to realize that privacy is important to people and that boundaries are essential to protect the "self" as well as those people moving within that individual's Universe.

It is possible that many emotional litterbugs have never separated completely from their mothers and continue to attempt to recreate the womblike atmosphere they enjoyed as children when love was the reward for honesty and punishment the consequence of secrecy. They believe that all people are good rather than bad, helpful rather than destructive, and supportive of the emotional litterbug's every interest and whim. These assumptions underlie their compulsive need to share thoughts ranging from the most mundane to the most intimate.

Those people in the emotional litterbug's immediate environment usually have little interest in getting closer. They immediately find themselves on privacy overload, tired of hearing everything about everybody, and upset at having their own secrets exposed.

Do you fall into this category? Do you have a highly permeable "self," which frequently discloses your secrets and those of others in hopes of creating intimate bonds?
Yes_____ No_____

THE GOSSIP GABBER

Angela was in charge of a secretarial pool for a large international conglomerate. To the women who worked under her, she behaved in a motherly fashion. When times were difficult, either personally or professionally, she urged her "girls" to share their problems with her. At first, they had been skeptical and responded only with bits of information but when Angela proved to be such a good listener, they opened up with more intimate confessions.

Eventually, Angela knew a great deal about each employee and, in time, used it to her advantage. When Michelle came to her one day, for example, and complained about Ruth, Angela closed her office door and quietly said, "Ruth is going through a terrible divorce. She just isn't herself. Be patient with her."

By sharing Ruth's secret with Michelle to keep the office running smoothly, Angela gained control over her two employees.

The months passed and Angela continued to reveal everyone's secrets when it suited her purpose, but always in "the strictest of confidence." She ended up creating a telephone-operator dynamic, reminiscent of the times when all calls went through a one-person switchboard in a small town, and the operator ended up knowing a great deal of personal information about each inhabitant.

Little by little, the secretaries, who had been kept apart by Angela's gossip, began to talk among themselves about their boss. They soon discovered that nothing they had said to Angela had remained a secret. Upset and betrayed, they began to clam up whenever Angela was around. The damage done to morale was significant, and productivity in the department suffered.

Finally, management discovered what had been going on and transferred Angela to another position, where she reported to one person rather than having many employees report to her.

Gossip gabbers like Angela need to be in control of as many people and situations as possible. Secrets become their weapons and are carefully used to manipulate others. Although gossip gabbers guard their own private world, they disregard others' by indiscriminately sharing their confidences. Under the guise of a "father" or "mother" confessor, the gossip gabber urges everyone to confide in him or her. If they don't, they are accused of being insecure about being known, a manipulative statement designed to make the other person feel inadequate and guilty.

When gossip gabbers are exposed, they usually act quite surprised. When charged with betraying the confidences of others, they are downright shocked. They can't imagine how they could have really hurt anyone by their maneuvering.

Does Angela's story set off identity bells for you? Do you have a permeable "self," which discloses other people's secrets to everyone all the time but keeps your actions and feelings private?
Yes_____ No_____

THE FRIENDLY EXTROVERT

Hayes, an exceptional student, was finishing work on his graduate degree in business. When it came time for him to enroll in an internship program, he turned to his most supportive professor. He realized that the proper introduction at this point could help him make contacts that would be helpful later on in his career.

Within a few weeks, Hayes's professor came through for him and lined him up with one of his friends in a Fortune 500 company. All went well until Hayes got involved in the new products division. He saw that its marketing manager, who was his professor's friend, was flying by the seat of his pants and that his staff was constantly covering for him. Disenchanted, Hayes went back to his professor, told him all, and asked for another recommendation.

He was shocked when he got a cold shoulder and the response "You make the change yourself."

It didn't take Hayes long to realize that he had made a drastic mistake. He had belittled the professor's friend and then expected the teacher to pick up the pieces. Hayes did move to another company but he had learned an important lesson. In the future, he vowed to be more careful about what feelings he revealed to whom and whose secrets he exposed.

Friendly extroverts like Hayes often feel pressured into telling their secrets because they want to be liked, understood, and accepted. Hayes, hoping to show off to his professor about having uncovered inefficient management, disregarded the feelings of loyalty the two men had developed over the years.

In the aftermath of the exposure, Hayes, like most friendly extroverts, felt apologetic about his actions.

Have you ever disclosed a secret and then regretted doing so? Would you say you have a permeable "self," which tends to reveal information to inappropriate people at times?
Yes____ No____

THE SECRET SAVVY PRO

Remember Clark and Grace, the happily married couple whom we met at the beginning of this chapter? They feared that they might be into sadomasochism because they had found that occasional spanking was sexually arousing.

When Clark called me and asked for some help, he mentioned that he didn't feel comfortable asking anyone else the question because another person might get the wrong impression and give the wrong information.

Clark was probably right. His decision is a good example of a secret savvy pro, the category that describes people who have well-developed secrecy/disclosure skills. They reveal their innermost thoughts and feelings in a nonimpulsive way and to appropriate people in the proper place at the right time.

An appropriate person is one who is well known to you: an individual who has been helpful in the past, will respond in an insightful manner, and one who will not misuse the confidence. It could be a recommended mental health professional. A proper place is quiet and private. And the right time is when neither person feels rushed with other matters — in essence, a time when you are mutually receptive to each others' needs.

Individuals with secret savvy, positioned as they are in the middle of the Secrecy/Disclosure Scale, rarely have problems with secrets. They know how to make concealing and revealing confidences a positive and enlightening experience.

Do you feel closely aligned with this category? Do you have a permeable "self," which usually reveals information to an appropriate person at the proper time and place? Do you know when to keep secrets? Do you utilize your secrets to gain insight into your personality and to improve your relationships? Yes___ No___

THE SHY INTROVERT

Jeremy, a single man in his late twenties, was feeling depressed and lonely because he couldn't meet anyone. "I go to parties and never seem to make contact," he told me over the phone during my radio program.

"Sounds like you prefer to stare at the ice rather than to break it," I joked.

"You're right," he said, admitting that he did feel more like looking at his drink than carrying on a conversation that would involve him in making some personal comments about himself. Jeremy added that his greatest fear was being rejected or laughed at by a stranger.

When Jeremy finally admitted that he had really been rejected only a few times, I suggested that he put his fears into perspective. Everyone is rejected from time to time. He needn't assume, I explained, anything more from the experience than that the relationship was not meant to be. Jeremy had begun to use automatic thoughts, a process whereby you try to read the other person's mind and you conclude that he or she does not like you.

"Are you shy, Jeremy?" I then asked.

"Very," he replied softly.

"Well, why not be open about your shyness? Let people know that social situations are difficult for you. I think you will find others to be very understanding and you won't be as tense after your revelation."

I didn't hear from Jeremy for a few weeks. Then he called back, saying that he had started to be more up-front with others about his shyness. He was surprised at how many people shared his problem.

Jeremy's dilemma is not unusual. Many of us have trouble walking into a room filled with unfamiliar faces, but most of us are able to initiate the introduction and begin talking to someone. We usually begin by making some small talk and disclosing a personal but not too private story about ourselves.

Shy introverts have difficulty striking up conversations with strangers because they feel uncomfortable about discussing even the most minor personal experience. They are terribly afraid of feeling foolish. No wonder they are told by others that initially they were hard to get to know.

Would you classify yourself as a shy introvert, someone with a slightly impermeable "self," who has problems disclosing anything of a personal nature to strangers or acquaintances?
Yes____ No____

THE GUARDED WITHHOLDER

Ted had barely returned from his honeymoon with Millie when he was given new responsibilities at work. His pleasure turned to anxiety almost immediately as he found himself over his head and frightened that he might be fired. To compensate for his inexperience, he started working late.

At home, Millie noticed how distant and moody her husband had become, but when she asked him what was wrong, he answered, "Nothing." Ted just couldn't bring himself to admit to her that he was in jeopardy of losing his job. As the pressure mounted at work and the backlog increased, Ted began working weekends. It was then that Millie concluded that only one thing could be keeping him so busy — another woman. Soon this couple, who had been so in love only months before, started silently to hate each other. She felt he was unfaithful. He thought she was critical and unsupportive.

Fortunately, they finally went into marriage counseling to see if they could save the relationship. At the first session, Millie blamed Ted for the problems and cried, "Why are you having an affair?"

Ted looked at his wife in shock and said he was doing nothing of the sort; that he loved her and no one else. "I'm having trouble at work," he admitted; "that's all. Get off my back!"

Now it was Millie's turn to be stunned. "Why didn't you tell me?"

"Why didn't you ask?"

"I couldn't ask because you were acting so obnoxious."

"I couldn't tell you because you were always so angry."

I listened to the rapid-fire blaming of each other and to why they had misinterpreted such an important communication. When the anger and tension had dissipated, I suggested that we investigate how guarded they had both been and why they had withheld information from one another.

Ted and Millie soon saw how lethal communication shutdowns could be. They reaffirmed their love for each other and promised to be more open in the future. They felt they had learned a good lesson.

Guarded withholders tend to strive for perfection in their lives and, like Ted and Millie, find it difficult to share their personal setbacks and insecurities with those most close. They are often misunderstood because they remain quiet and mysterious about what is happening in their lives. In time, their intimate relationships become stormy as partners and friends alike begin accusing them of not being open. These accusations leave the guarded withholder with confused and hurt feelings, which they also conceal.

Can you identify with this category? Do you have an impermeable "self," which finds it hard to disclose something to close friends and significant others if it exposes a less-than-perfect you? Yes____ No____

THE CLOSED-OFF CONCEALER

Remember Tom Milligan, whom we discussed in Chapter 2, the man who lived two separate lives and kept secrets from everyone? He was a closed-off concealer, and, like many in this category, probably had an extreme fear of getting close. By withholding information about himself, he took few interpersonal risks and, in that way, protected his image, maintained control, and remained separate from others.

When the fear of being hurt is carried to an extreme, especially if the person has been abused as a child, an adult emerges who verbally closes off in order to remain unknown. By building these walls, a person can deceive practically everybody and at the same time vent the anger that has built up about the abuse.

Milligan, for example, probably acted out some of his repressed rage (about what, we do not know) by fooling and belittling the townspeople with this "Rotarian of the Year" persona. He overtly released his pent-up hostility through his criminal behavior at night. As long as he was in charge and separate from everyone, he had few problems, but when his wife left him, he not only lost command of the situation but experienced rejection, which was something he had struggled to avoid. Killing her and her boyfriend was his ultimate reaction to being disapproved of and thrown out. After that, committing suicide probably seemed like the only option. His dual life-style was about to be exposed and then it was only a matter of time before he would be rejected by all.

Would you say that some of Milligan's feelings are similar to yours? Do you think that you have a highly impermeable "self," which finds it difficult to disclose anything about your life? Do you lead a secret life? Yes_____ No_____

Results

You probably found at least one person's case history that reminded you of yourself. Take a moment to reread the category or categories and understand why the individual tended to be open, balanced, or closed. Pay particular attention to the personality traits that person exhibits and why they place him or her at that particular point on the continuum. This information will give you more insight into your secrecy/disclosure nature and help you pinpoint the characteristics you might want to change.

The Secrecy/Disclosure Scale Quiz

Since you may have identified with more than one person in the Case History Quiz, you may be wondering in which category you really belong.

The Secrecy/Disclosure Scale Quiz will tell you that, because it will place you within one category based on how you reply to the questionnaire.

Take a pencil, read each question, and circle the number that best describes your response. The more specific you can be, the more accurate you will find your final results.

SECRECY/DISCLOSURE SCALE QUIZ

Code for numbers: 1 – almost always
2 – often
3 – sometimes
4 – seldom
5 – almost never

1. Others know a lot about my personal life because I tell them.

   1   2   3   4   5

2. I enjoy socializing.

   1   2   3   4   5

3. I tell the truth.

   1   2   3   4   5

4. Friends and family get angry because I can't keep secrets.

   1   2   3   4   5

5. When friends ask personal questions, I answer.

   1   2   3   4   5

6. I am outgoing.

   1   2   3   4   5

7. I think people want to hear what I have to say.

   1   2   3   4   5

8. I am friendly.

   1   2   3   4   5

9. After a social encounter, I feel as if I had said too much about myself.

   1   2   3   4   5

10. I find it easy to open up to others.

   1   2   3   4   5

11. I trust others.

   1   2   3   4   5

12. When strangers ask personal questions, I answer.

   1   2   3   4   5

13. I can't help talking about myself.

   1   2   3   4   5

14. Telling the truth is the most important consideration.

   1   2   3   4   5

15. I dislike being the quiet one in a relationship.

   1   2   3   4   5

Add the numbers that you have circled and subtract 5 from the total. Then note which category below covers your total and describes your secrecy/disclosure nature.

Emotional Litterbug   0–10
Gossip Gabber   10–20
Friendly Extrovert   20–30
Secret Savvy Pro   30–40
Shy Introvert   40–50
Guarded Withholder   50–60
Closed-off Concealer   60–70

Results

If you scored:

Between 0 and 20: You are either an emotional litterbug or a gossip gabber and will need to develop more self-control while working to establish a less permeable boundary between your "self" and your Universe. Impulsiveness is probably your worst enemy, equaled only by your need to please by telling people everything. You will want to start thinking more carefully before you reveal personal information about yourself and others.

Between 20 and 50: You are a friendly extrovert, are a secret savvy pro or can be classified as a shy introvert. You have fallen into a normal range of secret-keeping and secret-telling behavior. If your score is in the twenties and you are a friendly extrovert, you will want to be a little less impulsive than you are now when confronted with an opportunity to reveal a secret. Should you have scored in the forties and fit the definition of a shy introvert, you will need to consider opening up more and worrying less about the fear of social rejection.

Between 50 and 70: You are either a guarded withholder or a closed-off concealer, and rigidity is your nemesis, as is your desire to feel protected by remaining unknown to others. You will want to work on breaking down the rather impermeable boundary that is closing your "self" off from your Universe and find people with whom you feel safe because they will not misuse your confidences.

BEYOND THE BASICS

With the completion of these quizzes, you now know the type of secret-keeper or secret-teller you are. You are clear about whom you share your confidences with, how often you share, and what you do with other people's secrets. This information gives you a strong, clear bearing on your secret-handling nature.

Before you can begin to make any modifications you deem necessary, however, it would be beneficial to look back into your past to see how you became this way. Let's continue our journey by examining your seeds of secrecy/disclosure.

PART TWO

The Seeds of Secrecy/Disclosure

4

The Secretless and the Secret-shaping Years: Infancy to Age Five

NURSERY SCHOOL CHILDREN SEXUALLY ABUSED
Terrorized by Staff to Keep It Secret

THE headlines and news reports about child molesting have always been disturbing, but recently they have become horrifying to parents as day-care centers and nursery schools have been indicted. Although some cases have been dropped, others have been brought to trial.

One such tried case was Virginia McMartin's preschool in Manhattan Beach, California, where some 115 counts of child molestation were leveled originally against three McMartin family members and as many employees. Until the indictments, everyone assumed the school was aboveboard. Each day when parents dropped their children off at the entrance they dismissed their sons' or daughters' crying as growing-up pains. Little did the adults know that the tears may have been repressed anger and suppressed fears.

According to the newspaper accounts, once the school bell rang, the toddlers were led into the classroom and told to play games that were not on the curriculum. They were made to strip and stand by powerlessly as still and motion pictures were taken or as they themselves were driven off to other places, where strangers fondled them.

What appeared to be a normal preschool was eventually suspected of being an underground child pornography and prostitution outlet, and California law-enforcement authorities began to think that the preschool may have involved its young charges in everything from rape to oral sex.

When the indictments were finally made, people wondered how it could have happened and why the children didn't speak up. As the tots began to find their voices, everyone started to understand the reason they had remained silent. The staff apparently threatened the boys and girls by cutting up rabbits, squeezing birds to death, killing turtles, and then telling the children that their mothers and fathers would die similar deaths if anyone found out what was going on at school.

Parents were shocked, but soon admitted that they had misread all the signs, not only the redness in the vaginal and groin areas, but also the frightening dreams in the middle of the night and the wet beds.

You have probably identified from the last two symptoms that these two-to-five-year-olds were suffering from secrecy strain and its adverse side effects, from hypersensitivity to the fear of being found out. This was dramatically shown after one boy described what occurred by using a Pac-Man puppet. When he had finished telling his story of sexual abuse, he put the puppet down and said, "Pac-Man's dead. He told the secret."

Are you surprised that children so young are aware of and influenced by secrecy? Actually most of the preschoolers were too immature in their growth and development to grasp the concept consciously. Still, they acquiesced to remaining quiet, and in the process learned about secretive behavior because of their natural dependence on their parents. The tots believed that if their mothers and fathers died they themselves would not be able to survive. By refusing to say a word, they "bargained" that their parents would be spared and their own lives saved.

The seeds of secrecy/disclosure, as you can see from this example, can be planted early. Your own initiation was influenced by your parents' personalities, punishment-and-reward systems, and your gender. These factors also helped shape your present-day too open or too closed nature.

SEEDS OF SECRECY/DISCLOSURE: THE CONCEPTION

Your seeds of secrecy/disclosure did not simply bloom with your first secret. They really began to grow and be tended soon after birth. By the time you reached the beginning of adolescence and had passed through the stages of infancy, early childhood, childhood, and preadolescence, the seeds had grown so that you were either using secrets in a satisfying manner or finding the whole business of keeping and sharing confidences disconcerting.

Let's look at all the phases you went through from birth to age eighteen and see what you learned about secrecy and disclosure and what role they played in your life. This should be most revealing, because in each stage it was important that you performed certain tasks that would enable you to develop a balanced nature. If you missed a task or became rooted in one stage because you were frightened by a particular task, that experience could have prevented you from maturing into a secret savvy pro.

INFANCY: BIRTH TO EIGHTEEN MONTHS, A SECRETLESS TIME

You are born with a totally permeable "self." The skill to distinguish between that "self" and the outside world will come only with time. Your thinking is not well developed enough for secrecy to affect your world. You do not have the aptitude to remember or to feel a sense of wrongdoing, and you could not conceptualize the possibility of telling someone something, even if you had the ability to speak.

Stumbling Blocks of Infancy

It is difficult to determine how your secrecy/disclosure nature is influenced during infancy, but there is a series of identifiable obstacles that hamper your natural maturation and in turn can affect your secret-concealing and secret-revealing future. Those stumbling blocks are lack of self-esteem, the tense-mother syndrome, and the perils of an extended ideal infancy.

LACK OF SELF-ESTEEM

When you are an infant, your initial taste of what the world is like comes from your interaction with others. If you are fed and changed in a predictable manner and cared for with love, you tend to develop a sense that you are worthwhile because your physical demands are unconditionally met. This experience translates into an evolving self-esteem, a trait that favorably affects your ability to tell or keep secrets eventually in an appropriate way.

According to clinical psychologists who have researched the correlation between self-concept and self-disclosure, subjects who were high in self-esteem could be expected to be comparatively high (but not too high) in self-disclosing behavior.

THE TENSE-MOTHER TRAUMA

If your mother was anxious about many things in her life, you may have felt that tenseness and interpreted it to mean that the world was a bad place. Your "reading" may have led you to feel unsure about how to get along in that confusing environment and may have been the beginning of your pattern of being too secretive. As an adult you may be inclined to be distrustful and to fall on the closed end of the Secrecy/Disclosure Scale.

THE PERILS OF AN EXTENDED IDEAL INFANCY

All infancies should be idyllic, with the baby dependent on the parent for every need, but if this relationship goes on for too long, then problems can occur. Should your mother, for example, not have fostered a little separation as you were about to move out of this stage at about eighteen months, you may still be somewhat stuck in it, striving for a motherlike bond with others.

This kind of upbringing usually breeds emotional litterbugs. Telling secrets becomes their connection with people. They trust everyone and expect that their needs will be met once the other person knows their confidence.

The Main Task

By eighteen months, although you are still basically innocent as far as secrecy is concerned, you have stored away many impressions that will affect your secrecy/disclosure nature. You have discovered whether or not you are worthwhile, whether the world is a relatively safe or a dangerous place, whether people can be trusted, and whether you deserve to be treated well.

The farther you emerge from this stage of trusting your parents, especially your mother, the easier it is to move on to the next phase and the less likely you are to have potential problems dealing with secrets.

Trust, then, is the primary secrecy/disclosure task to be learned in infancy, and the best teacher is a relatively relaxed and reliable caretaking adult.

EARLY CHILDHOOD: EIGHTEEN MONTHS TO FIVE YEARS, A SECRET-SHAPING TIME

Once you enter early childhood you need to develop a more impermeable "self." This is the period when you begin to lay the groundwork for secret savvy by experiencing yourself as separate from others. Your parents help you with separation by requiring you to control your behavior in two significant ways: through toilet training and obedience.

The ability to control your bodily functions gives you the opportunity to please your mother and father, whom you still need and love. If you are successful because their standards are not too high, and if they rely on rewards rather than punishment, you can come out of this stage pleased with yourself and possessing heightened self-esteem. You will be more likely to grow up feeling lovable, certain that the world is safe, and capable of exerting control. These beliefs help you form the confidence that is essential in shaping the balanced secret-handling nature.

If the opposite occurs, and your parents continually resort to shaming and punishment, you will tend to feel less confident in general. As an adult, you may be afraid of making mistakes or of being found imperfect. These feelings could push you toward a rather private life, based on a fear that if people really knew you, they would reject you much as your parents did when you were unable to control your bowels.

As your verbal ability and physical agility increase, you are introduced to your parents' dos and don'ts. These limitations come when you are finally ready to rebel against authoritarian control. This rebelliousness during the "terrible twos" is summed up in one dramatic and usually earsplitting answer: "No!"

When you find that your needs start to differ from what your parents want for you, conflict begins to arise. Since you are now starting to feel more separate than ever from your mother and father, you think your desires are extremely important and must be fulfilled. At this point, you are also initially sensing what is right and wrong, as well as what can upset your parents. A problem is created because you are yearning for more independence at a time when you are still actually very dependent, so you don't really want to drastically offend anyone you need. In order to get or do as much as possible with the least chance of punishment or rejection, you develop an alert system known as signal anxiety.

This internal warning circuit helps you anticipate conflicts between you and your parents whether or not you recognize that what you are doing is naughty. Signal anxiety may be triggered by a parental look or by the vibrations you feel in a threatening situation similar to one where you were previously spanked or sent to your room.

When the "bell" goes off you go into action either by avoiding the threat or by attempting to take charge by saying "No." You have not yet learned to hide your behavior, because you are certain your parents have a magical talent for reading your innermost thoughts and can tell from the expression on your face that you have misbehaved.

Your First Secret

One day something happens to change all that. Perhaps you break a glass or tear a piece of clothing. In a panic, stimulated by signal anxiety and a growing conscience, you bury the pieces deep in the trash or toss the evidence far under the bed so the act won't be discovered and you can avoid punishment. The episode escapes parental eyes and, as the days pass, you continue to say nothing. Your fear of being found out diminishes as the incident slips into the past and your mother and father remain oblivious. You soon realize that you have controlled what your parents know about you. Suddenly you feel more in charge of your life and more separate from your parents, a sensation that results in growing self-esteem.

Once you successfully withhold information from either your mother or father, you discover one of the positive rewards of secret-keeping — preventing punishment or rejection.

At the same time that you begin to make secrets work for you they start to work against you. This is when you are exposed to the negative side effects of secretive behavior. You begin to realize that keeping a confidence to yourself forces you to live in fear of discovery. This realization puts you in a conflict cycle for each secret that you have, and you remain there until the confidence is revealed.

As a child you may be involved in several conflict cycles at one time. The number that you get stuck in during this phase of your

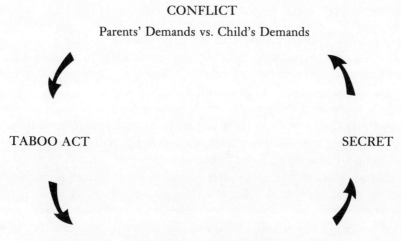

CONFLICT

Parents' Demands vs. Child's Demands

TABOO ACT   SECRET

INTERNAL CONFLICT

Child's Fear of Discovery and Punishment/Rejection

The Conflict Cycle. Your parents' demands differ from yours, and that fact creates a conflict. When you do something contrary to their wishes, you again become conflicted because you fear discovery will lead to punishment or rejection. You decide that keeping the act a secret will protect you from being found out. Since your parents' demands do not change nor do yours, you continue to differ from them, think about the taboo act, consider the consequences of discovery and feel anxious, keep your secret, remember how your demands differ from your parents', and so on. . . . You will continue to revolve in this cycle until you tell your secret.

growth and development is determined by your parents' handling of your socialization process. The more loving and supportive your mother and father are and the less they use excessive punishment, the fewer internal conflicts you will experience.

A certain amount of secretive conflict in your life is normal. Problems arise, however, if you are caught up in too many conflict cycles. When you are an adult, these past involvements can dramatically influence your secrecy/disclosure nature either by encouraging the indiscriminate telling of secrets or by stimulating withholding behavior. You are closed because you have had no experience in revealing secrets or you are open because you want to avoid the anxiety of the conflict cycle as you remember it.

The Parental Factor

Your parents' personalities and reactions throughout early childhood greatly influence how you view the outside world.

During this period your mother and father need to set limits in a sensible, nonrigid manner, be relaxed about their own sexuality and yours, and be quick to act as a buffer for you against external forces.

If they are nurturing in those ways, you are more likely to pass through this phase with a maturing sense of trust and an appropriate degree of openness. The growth of these traits will be helping you develop a balanced secret-handling nature.

Should, however, your mother or father have a serious problem, such as an alcohol addiction; should you be left on your own too frequently or at too young an age; should you be shamed and punished continuously when you do something wrong or make a mistake — you will probably come out of this stage guarded, closed, and suspicious of the world and the people in it.

On the other hand, if your parents don't let you grow up and make friends outside the family but keep you close to them and too dependent, you may come out of this stage too open, with a tendency to treat the whole world as though it has your best interests at heart.

To show you how crucial your parents' reactions to you can be and how their personalities and punishment techniques can harm you if they are too negative and rigid, let me tell you about a girl named Stephanie. She was suicidal when she entered my office, said she was twenty-five and was having an affair with a married man while she was living with her female lover.

Stephanie explained that neither lover knew of the other's existence. Then she smiled with delight. She told me how much she loved to have many secrets in her life. They gave it drama and enabled her to shock people whenever she took them into her confidence.

As we delved into Stephanie's childhood over the next two years, I uncovered a little girl who had had a most difficult upbringing. Her mother was an alcoholic and her father rarely came home. She had no friends, and to escape from this unhappy world she created imaginary playmates, a quite normal reaction for a lonely young child.

Stephanie's mother, however, made her feel abnormal by acting shocked that she would play with dolls as if they were real people. After being shamed and laughed at several times by her mother, Stephanie started to fantasize with her "friends" in secret. (I later discovered that this berating was the only time Stephanie received any type of parental attention.)

When Stephanie went to school she made few friends because she preferred to play with her dolls. She could control them, unlike the real children, who demanded to visit her home and meet her mother. Stephanie, fearing her parents' anger and her schoolmates' laughter, withdrew from the playground and avoided all invitations. She had begun to live a guarded life.

As a teenager, Stephanie started turning her doll-created fantasies into real-life adventures. Now her "playmates" were flesh and blood, but since she knew the "script" she felt no danger. She was in control.

She got the greatest thrill out of shocking a person who thought he or she knew her well. Stephanie thrived on these situations that were throwbacks to the recognition she had always received from her mother when she had been shocked by her daughter's behavior.

During the therapy sessions, Stephanie saw how her mother's shaming of her natural fantasy playtime had driven it underground and caused her to begin a secret life.

Stephanie also looked at why she wanted to do away with herself. She started to realize that she was lonely and desperate because she had never learned to relate to anyone on an intimate level. Stephanie had to learn as an adult what most people learn as children: that closeness comes only with vulnerability and trust, and that we all must live in a real world. Another thing she began to understand in therapy was that she didn't have to shock others with her secrets to feel loved.

Today Stephanie is no longer existing on the edge. Her life is more tranquil and she is not controlling her friends' lives. She is pursuing an ambition to be on the stage, a place where she can enjoy make-believe without having it infringe on her reality.

As Stephanie's case history indicates, the way you treat secrets as an adult can be influenced by your parents' personalities and reactions to you. A rigid home environment or parents beset with behavioral problems can contribute to a nature that is too closed. A family where you are kept dependent on your mother or father can lead to a nature that is too open. It is when you are raised in a relaxed atmosphere where trust is fostered and your parents become buffers against the outside world that the nature you develop tends to be balanced.

The Gender Factor

During early childhood your gender begins to play a significant role in how open or closed you are becoming. Carol Gilligan, an expert at Harvard University in the psychological growth and development of women, has spearheaded a movement to understand the repercussions of growing up female or male. In her book *In a Different Voice*, she wrote that early on, girls find intimate relationships natural and reveal more of themselves than boys do because they feel that attachment signifies something that is good, warm, and loving. Even in childhood, boys find separateness more comfortable.

It would therefore follow, from the research of Ms. Gilligan and others, that men tend to have a more closed nature than women. This finding gives you another key as to your ranking on the Secrecy/Disclosure Scale.

MOVING ON

As you passed through infancy and early childhood your seeds of secrecy/disclosure were beginning to grow. They were being tended by your parents' personalities, punishment-and-reward system, and your gender.

When you left these two stages you had a certain degree of trust, a belief that the world was a safe place, and the assurance that you had the ability to control at least some aspects of your world.

The more secure you felt in these three areas at this phase of your life, the more likely it is that you were developing a balanced secrecy/disclosure nature.

5

The Secret-Safety and the Secret-healing Years: Ages Five to Thirteen

JIMMY sneaked into the corner store, and, when Mr. Archer, the owner, wasn't looking, snatched a chocolate bar. Moments later he was outside the shop, candy in hand and a smile on his face. He had his favorite treat without having had to pay for it.

Arriving home, Jimmy tossed the unopened candy into his dresser drawer. The thrill of the theft was gone, and now he felt a bit guilty. Deciding it would be best if no one knew what he had done, he vowed to play safe and keep it a secret.

A few days passed, and as Jimmy's mother was putting away his underwear, she noticed the wrapped chocolate bar. She was immediately suspicious, because her son loved candy and under normal circumstances would have devoured this bar as soon as he bought it.

That evening Jimmy's mother asked him how he had come to purchase the chocolate. She knew he was already in debt to his father and wouldn't be getting any allowance for another week.

Jimmy didn't say a word, but he felt uneasy. Then he heard his mother's words, "If you tell me the truth, you won't be punished and I will always love you."

Figuring that all would be forgiven and forgotten, Jimmy confessed. He was horrified when he learned that his mother wanted him to return the candy even though he had told her the truth. He had been tricked. He pleaded with her to let the incident pass and then argued that he had told his secret only to avoid punishment. Jimmy's mother was unmoved, saying that he had done something wrong and needed to make amends to Mr. Archer. She did agree, though, to go with him to the store for moral support.

Mr. Archer listened carefully to Jimmy's apology and admonished him for having taken the candy. He said, however, that since Jimmy had returned it he would overlook the episode and not call the police. Jimmy breathed a sigh of relief and never noticed how Mr. Archer winked at his mother who was herself smiling, assured that her seven-year-old had learned an important lesson about devious behavior.

CHILDHOOD: AGES FIVE TO EIGHT, SECRET-SAFETY

Jimmy's antisocial behavior is one example of how we all strive during childhood to be more independent from our parents even though we realize that we cannot survive without them and that we also need their love and approval.

This is a stage when you are looking for a way to assert yourself by rebelling not only against your mother and father but against new authority figures that come into your life. Although you continue to build upon your disclosure skills, your focus is on secrecy.

Secrets become an ally in childhood, and the task you are to learn in this phase is how to conceal and reveal information when you are with your parents and other authorities, such as teachers. You are ready to take this step because your language and thinking skills have developed along with your knowledge of what meets your parents' and other superiors' approval.

Secrecy's Trial Balloons

There are four childhood events in which you test your ability to be independent and experiment with secrecy to achieve your goal. Those experiences are stealing, masturbation, truancy, and sibling rivalry. They reflect the main aspects of your environment at this stage: unattainable objects, pleasure, school, and competition for parental love.

Since these activities deal with socially unacceptable behavior for a child, your mother and father, as well as other authority figures, are either understanding or punitive.

The way you handle each event, the role secrecy plays in it, and the reaction you receive for your revelations or concealments have an effect on your maturing secretive nature.

STEALING

Jimmy's case history indicates how the act of stealing can be an attempt by a child to get something without having to rely on someone else. It may also be an unconscious ploy to test parental control.

Although Jimmy hid what he had done, his mother uncovered his secret. Her reaction was supportive rather than abusive, but she made it a point to tell him that he had done something wrong and would have to admit it.

MASTURBATION

By the time you are five years old, you have discovered your body and are probably enjoying the sensations that masturbation can arouse. Having reached childhood, you need to learn that this pleasurable act is to be performed privately.

One night while Jason's parents were giving a dinner party, he began rubbing himself against a balustrade on the center hall staircase. Although his mother was embarrassed, she did not make a scene. Instead, she excused herself and took Jason to his room. Once there, she did not shame, reject, or punish him. She understood his natural urge. She did, though, help Jason understand why masturbation should be done in private.

This incident helped Jason realize that sexual acts are to be enjoyed in privacy and that those experiences should be kept secret.

TRUANCY

As with stealing, truancy is a way to rebel against parental control as well as against an authority figure of a new kind, the teacher. When you skip school in childhood you tend to do it with friends because the shared experience is a lot more fun.

Take Patricia, for example. She and three girlfriends decided to play hookey. They met several blocks from the school, books and lunch bags in hand, and proceeded to a densely wooded area, where they giggled as they watched from their vantage point the other children working on their lessons. Patricia and her friends felt a heady sense of control and a strong alliance with each other at that moment.

The girls were never caught and they soon tired of these periodic adventures. The secret acts had served their purpose. The girls had learned to share confidences with each other in a trusting atmosphere luckily without suffering any consequences.

SIBLING RIVALRY

The fourth antisocial experience of your childhood is the negative feelings you have for your brothers or sisters. Some of these feelings come about because of rivalry for parental love. Others arise at times when you find that your siblings interfere with your peer relations. If your brother or sister is very different from other kids, for instance, you may attempt to dissociate yourself from that sibling to protect your image. Secrets become your bedfellow.

Tod was seven years old when he started telling his friends that he was an only child. He did this because he was embarrassed by his older brother, Keith, who had been born with a brain dysfunction that caused him to be physically slow and socially awkward.

At first everyone believed Tod. They did think it was odd that they were never invited to his house, although he came to theirs, but they didn't press the issue. Then one day, Peter found out about Keith and confronted his friend with the truth. Tod convinced him to keep the discovery a secret.

This case history indicates how secrecy can be helpful in childhood. Being secretive enabled Tod to handle the embarrassment he felt about his brother at school and the resentment he harbored toward Keith at home. The secrecy pact that Tod made with Peter created a special bond between them and taught them both about sharing a secret.

Our story about Tod, Keith, and Peter does not end here but moves on as they matured into preadolescence. You will be able to follow the situation to its conclusion when we discuss the next stage of growth and development.

Jimmy, Jason, Patricia, and Tod experienced the positive benefits of secrecy because they used secrets without receiving negative reactions from their parents or another authority figure. Their experiments with concealing and revealing information were helping them build toward a balanced secrecy/disclosure nature.

Think back to when you were around six or seven years of age. You probably were involved in all these socially unacceptable acts. The way your mother and father handled these incidents affected how you deal with secrecy as an adult.

For example, if your parents discovered your secret and pulled you up short but in a loving and supportive way, they proved that although you would not be seriously punished you would have to face up to the situation. By setting limits on antisocial behavior, they may have stopped such actions in the future. Their understanding but realistic reaction could also have made you feel secure about later telling your secrets to close friends and your spouse. You would probably assume that others would respond like your mother and father.

If your parents ignored your socially unacceptable actions, you may have felt that you had the upper hand and a real talent for getting away with things. You may have been tempted to try more antisocial behavior as you grew up and were attracted to a peer group where such acts were praised. Now, in adulthood, you could find that you continue to break rules and then use secrets as a coverup. With your underdeveloped conscience, you will tend to handle secrecy and disclosure in a self-destructive manner.

Should your mother or father have severely reprimanded you and then withheld their love which you desperately needed, you may have decided to tell them everything you did that was wrong and now, as an adult tend to be very open about your inadequacies.

Parental Behavior

While you are keeping and telling secrets at this stage, your parents are not only reacting to you but teaching you as well. The way they deal with secrecy and disclosure affects you.

If your mother and father tended to be closed, guarded and suspicious you may imitate that behavior. Should they have been too open, you are likely to err in that direction.

Secrecy Breeds Independence

When you reach the end of childhood, around the age of eight, you have begun to discover how secrecy can make you feel in control of your life, separate from your parents and close to your friends. If you have learned this stage's secrecy task — how to protect yourself from authorities — and have not suffered severe parental punishing or lack of interest, you will be developing a balanced nature. You will also be better prepared for the next phase, preadolescence, where you can experience secrecy and disclosure as a freeing and healing force that has the power to minimize the effect of past traumatic incidents.

PREADOLESCENCE: AGES EIGHT TO THIRTEEN, SECRET-HEALING

"You're my best and only friend."

If there is one phrase synonymous with your preteenage years, this is the one. It may already have brought back memories of a person from whom you were inseparable, an individual most likely of the same sex, with whom you shared everything.

In the preadolescent stage, your parents' importance diminishes as you grow in your confidence about your ability to survive on your own. As you move slowly away from their support system, you initially select a group of friends to lean on. That camaraderie is eventually replaced by one person of the same sex because it feels as if that person is safer than a member of the opposite sex. After all, he or she is more like you and consequently easier to know and understand.

The Friendly Group

At first, you learn about the outside world and other people's lives by being in a clique of friends, where you experiment with revealing and concealing private information. It is essential that your parents allow you to be part of that group and honor your need for privacy. If they don't, you presently may find yourself deficient in the skills you need for a balanced secrecy/disclosure nature.

Priscilla, a colleague of mine, told me an interesting story when she heard I was writing this book. She said that one of the reasons she was attracted to the profession of psychotherapy was that she had rarely heard any secrets during her preadolescence.

It seems that Priscilla's mother refused to let her have slumber parties because she felt their home couldn't compare to the houses of the other girls. As a result, Priscilla was excluded from a major experience of secret-sharing.

Not having the opportunity to share or hear peer secrets, Priscilla felt left out and inferior to her friends. This uncomfortable feeling stayed with her into adulthood and seemed to be a factor that influenced her career choice. Today Priscilla spends hours listening to her clients divulge their most private thoughts.

In a way Priscilla is making up for the secrets she didn't hear as a preteenager. As we talked further, I also discovered that she admits to making mistakes at times when dealing with her own secrets. A common problem for her is disclosing something to an inappropriate person.

Priscilla agreed with me that on the Secrecy/Disclosure Scale she is probably a friendly extrovert in need of being less impulsive with disclosure.

"TO ONE ANOTHER BE TRUE"

Developing your secrecy/disclosure skills within a group is one aspect of preadolescence, but the most important task of this stage is learning how to share personal information mutually with one other person of your sex. By risking true intimacy, you strive to be fully known and accepted, and in the process you attempt to understand yourself better. This reciprocal disclosure can be most beneficial; in fact, it can help heal past traumas, modify your personality, and allow for cross-healing.

These experiences can occur because no matter how open or closed you have become you will find yourself receptive at this stage to changing your secret-handling nature and your general emotional self. You are on a springboard about to leap into events that will bring on adulthood. The conflicts of childhood are behind you and the biological and psychological eruptions of adolescence are waiting in the wings. You are in a quiet, open-minded, transitional phase and about to experience how potentially therapeutic revealing secrets can be.

SECRETS PLUS APPROPRIATE DISCLOSURE EQUAL HEALING

Tina discovered the healing power of shared secrets when she was twelve years old and went away to camp with her best friend, Cara.

Late one night the two girls began taking turns telling intimate secrets. When Tina's turn came for the third time, she burst into tears. Cara reached over to give her a hug but instead, Tina handed her a diary. By the time Cara had read just a few pages, she understood why her friend was so upset.

An only child, Tina had always been the "mother" in the family because her own was often ill and frequently bedridden. When Tina was about ten, her mother was taken to the hospital for a major operation. Left at home with her father, Tina continued her mothering role. One night that role turned to wife as her father came into her room and found her clad only in her underwear. Aroused, he sexually assaulted her.

During the month while Tina's mother was recovering in the hospital, her father continued his sexual abuse. It didn't even stop when his wife returned home. Tina was too frightened to tell anyone; in fact, she began withdrawing from her friends. She felt the whole thing was her fault. She shouldn't have let her father see her in her underwear.

Cara sat on the bunk bed for some time after finishing the diary and held her sobbing friend in her arms. She reassured Tina that it was not her fault. No father, she said, should do anything like that to his daughter. The words soothed Tina and made her feel less guilty.

Upon returning home, Cara, thinking that perhaps her friend needed protection from her father as well as counseling, told her mother what had happened. Her mother immediately set up an appointment for Tina with the school psychologist. Soon Tina's mother found out. She was appalled. She had always known that the marriage had not been good for her, but she had no idea that Tina was suffering as well. She became determined to file for divorce.

After a year in therapy, Tina felt considerably calmer and no longer blamed herself for her father's actions. She also felt safer and had more confidence in her ability to judge people. These factors helped her change her secrecy/disclosure nature from being closed to being more balanced. The psychologist attributed the beginning of improvement in Tina's mental health to her sharing her secret with Cara. If Tina had kept that secret to herself, she could have carried her negative feelings about herself and men into adulthood and, like many incest victims, suffered the consequences years later.

SECRETS PLUS APPROPRIATE DISCLOSURE EQUAL PERSONALITY MODIFICATION

When you share a secret with a best friend during this stage, there is an opportunity for your personality difficulties to be modified.

Remember Tod, who denied the existence of his brain-damaged brother for fear he would be considered weird through association? Here is the rest of the story.

Peter, the friend who agreed to keep Tod's secret, began to feel guilty, especially when he saw how painful the secret was for Keith. When he encouraged Tod to drop the charade, Tod flew into a rage. No one could know, he said, what he was going through at home and how much personal jealousy and upset Keith had caused him.

He explained that he got very little attention from his parents, who thought Keith needed it all. This lack of attention left Tod feeling like an outsider in his own home. Acknowledging Keith to his friends could only make matters worse. He would certainly be rejected at school, and then he wouldn't have anybody.

Peter empathized with Tod's feelings but reassured him that the kids at school would continue to like him for who he was and wouldn't reject him because of his brother. He also pointed out that some of his classmates had already found out about Keith and were starting to think less of Tod.

Peter's caring confrontation helped his friend. Tod realized he was wrong. Soon everyone knew that he and Keith were related. Now that Tod was less guarded, he invited kids to his home and his friendships grew. His relationships with his parents improved too when they saw how he and Keith were getting along much better.

Tod had finally realized that he would be judged on his own merit. He had also discovered that parental love and support were not the only important type of nurturance available. In addition, he learned that sharing a secret with a good friend can change you for the better.

SECRETS PLUS APPROPRIATE DISCLOSURE EQUAL CROSS-HEALING

Modifying behavior traits for the better with secrets doesn't have to be one-sided. In fact, there can be cross-healing when two friends set about helping each other with their problems.

Everyone at school assumed Audrey was neat as a pin in all ways because she came to classes daily looking as if she had just stepped off the cover of a fashion magazine. They also believed that her best friend, Betsy, had a perfect relationship with her mother because they were so "cute" together in public.

In reality, Audrey was a slob. Her room at home resembled a combat zone. Clothes were piled high, papers were scattered about, food lay in varying stages of decay, and her bed was made only when the sheets were changed.

Betsy had created another kind of facade. She had a terrible relationship with her mother. They were always arguing.

The two girls knew each other's secrets and spent a lot of time talking about their respective problems.

Betsy asked Audrey why she appeared one way at school but lived in a completely different manner. Audrey finally came to the conclusion that she really didn't feel as "together" as she looked. She dressed and undressed many times every morning before she left for school. She feared she would be rejected if she didn't look just right.

Betsy reminded her that few people feel "together" all the time and that even famous people are afraid of rejection. Audrey's conversation with Betsy helped her relax a little. She decided to try to be less of a perfectionist in her dress and to see how it felt to live with more order at home.

Betsy then shared with Audrey her real feelings about her mother. She complained about how demanding and unloving the mother was and how the only thing that was important to her was the family's image.

Audrey reminded her friend that her mother was under a lot of pressure to support the family and that the stress obviously was making her short-tempered. Betsy shrugged her shoulders and responded that she was tired of trying to understand her mother. Audrey countered that by being sympathetic to and understanding of her mother's situation, she might be able to cool down the confrontations.

Betsy wasn't sure about Audrey's idea but decided to give it a try. She promised that she would be less argumentative with her mother and anytime Audrey observed her forgetting her promise, if she would say the word *attitude*, Betsy would check herself.

After a few months, the word *attitude* appeared less and less in the conversation while the two girls were together at Betsy's home. The relationship between Betsy and her mother improved.

In this instance, both girls helped each other resolve their secret problems. Without that healing friendship, Audrey might have become even more perfectionistic and Betsy could have carried her anger toward her mother into her future relationships.

Truth Sessions

Tina and Cara, Tod and Peter, and Audrey and Betsy indicate why preadolescence may be defined best as a stage of truth sessions. They each found that the clique was important but that an intimate same-sex friendship was essential. By sharing a good deal of private information with one another they were able to heal a past trauma, modify a personality difficulty, and cross-heal. They also became more appropriately open.

If your experience with mutual disclosure in this stage is a positive one, you can be reassured that you are developing a balanced secrecy/disclosure nature. Should you be hurt by a friend or not have one at all, you will emerge from this phase deficient in certain secrecy/disclosure skills. In the future you will discover intimate relationships are troublesome and sharing personal information is problematic.

THE NEXT STEP

In the secret-safety and secret-healing years, you have been exposed to learning two secrecy/disclosure tasks: how to protect yourself from authorities and how to have a more intimate peer relationship with healing potential.

When you are around thirteen years of age, you take what skills you have and enter a most demanding stage, adolescence. There you will complement what you have learned with four new secrecy/disclosure tasks and in the process put the finishing touches on your adult secret-handling nature.

6

The Secret-for-All-Reasons Years: Ages Thirteen to Eighteen

"I fainted at my high school graduation."

His voice was tense as he continued. "I was walking down the aisle to my seat, and I got dizzy. My knees just buckled under me, and the next thing I knew I was coming to backstage in the auditorium. My civics teacher was giving me a drink of water. She was saying that I could go on the stage from there and get my diploma when my name was called.

"The kids were staring at me. I was so embarrassed that I didn't finish the water. I got up and ran out. I still don't have my diploma and I'm nineteen."

When Lewis stopped talking, I asked him what had prompted this call to an advice radio program after more than two years since the incident.

"I'm afraid I'm ill," he replied. "I haven't gone to a doctor but I think my fainting was the first sign of some terrible disease."

"It sounds like graduation was a traumatic experience for you," I responded, attempting to see if the blackout had been psychologically or physically induced.

After my question, Lewis began to open up. He explained that high school was difficult for him because his parents had divorced when he was fifteen and the split left him feeling responsible and rejected. He recounted how his mother had devoted her time to his two younger sisters and how his father, who had remarried shortly after the divorce, had made it clear that Lewis was not welcome to live with him.

Lewis said that feeling like an outcast, he had left home, rented a room not far from school, and made ends meet by working in a department store. He bought food at a corner delicatessen and cooked over a hot plate that he had purchased.

At school, Lewis gave everyone the impression that he lived in a happy home. To make sure that this belief continued, he did not become close to anyone for fear his secret would be uncovered. He further protected himself by telling his classmates that his parents worked two jobs and were unable to attend various school activities.

"I wanted to be like all the other kids," he added, "those who had mothers and fathers, and belonged to a regular family."

"Did your parents come to your graduation?" I asked.

"No. I couldn't ask them. I figured that if I invited both, neither would come, and if I only asked one, the other wouldn't ever speak to me again. So I didn't send them invitations. Of course, my problem wasn't solved. I knew the kids would wonder where my parents were and then I would be exposed unless I lied."

His story appeared to be over, but I asked if he was still living as he had in high school. I wasn't surprised to hear him answer yes. He also said that he continued to feel terrible about his parents' divorce, which is why he had told no one, until he called me, that he was from a broken home.

I suggested that he get a physical examination but reassured him that I didn't think he was ill. I thought he was probably suffering the effects of keeping so many secrets for so long. Attempting to maintain a facade was debilitating, physically as well as emotionally. His fear of being discovered may have triggered his body to *give out* so he wouldn't have to *give up* his secrets.

We then discussed how many teenagers come from broken homes and how the ending of a marriage isn't a child's fault but the result of a husband's and wife's relationship that goes awry.

Just talking about his secrets helped Lewis put his situation into better perspective. He realized how isolating himself from his friends had prevented them from helping him deal with his situation and kept him from understanding that others were in the same predicament.

When we finished talking, Lewis said he felt relieved. He decided to call his high school for his diploma and to begin working on being more open with people about his personal life.

ADOLESCENCE: THIRTEEN TO EIGHTEEN YEARS, SECRETS FOR ALL REASONS

Between your thirteenth and eighteenth birthdays, you go through many physical, emotional, intellectual, and sexual changes. At times, your world no longer seems within your control. You have trouble defining who you really are and what is important.

Secrecy and disclosure continue to be essential, and you use both for all reasons: to avoid rejection by your peers, as Lewis did, to prevent punishment from your parents and other authorities, and to create bonds with friends of both sexes.

This is a most fascinating period, a time when you are building upon what you have learned about yourself, other people, the outside world, and secrecy and disclosure.

Before we delve into these years and their effect on your secret-keeping and secret-telling behavior, let's see what you remember about this stage of your life. Take out your pencil, make believe you are sixteen years old, and start answering the following questions with either a T for "True" or an F for "False."

1. _____ I think of myself as friendly.
2. _____ Other kids trust me with their secrets.
3. _____ A best friend knows my most important secret(s).
4. _____ If I tell someone a secret and they tell others, I don't want that person as a friend, especially if it happens more than once.
5. _____ I rarely tell other kids' secrets to friends or acquaintances.
6. _____ There are certain secrets I haven't told *anyone*.
7. _____ I tell my parent(s) or another adult more secrets than I share with my best friend.
8. _____ Friends don't tell me many of their secrets.

9. _____ I tell more secrets to opposite-sex friends than same-sex friends.

10. _____ Telling other kids' secrets sometimes gets me in trouble.

11. _____ I have at least two good friends.

12. _____ I keep a diary.

13. _____ I know which of my friends' secrets to keep and which to tell.

14. _____ I think of myself as popular.

15. _____ I think carefully about the pros and cons before I share one of my own secrets with a friend.

16. _____ I want to be liked.

17. _____ I spend at least one hour daily on the telephone with friends.

18. _____ I know most of my friends' secrets.

19. _____ Mere acquaintances sometimes tell me secrets.

20. _____ If there was a secret that I couldn't tell anyone and that was bothering me a lot, I would talk to a counselor, doctor, or clergyman.

I have experienced the following and have kept them a secret:

21. _____ suicidal thoughts or acts

22. _____ vomiting or other unnatural acts intended to lose weight

23. _____ episodes of gorging food

24. _____ insomnia or panic attacks

25. _____ sexually bizarre activities

26. _____ abuse (sexual or physical harm)

SCORING: Give yourself one point for each "True" answer among the following questions: numbers 1–5 and 11–20, and one point for each "False" answer to questions 6–10 and 21–26. Total the points and read on.

If you scored:

21–26: Your teen years were basically ones in which secrecy and disclosure were not a big problem. You were able to get along with most people, were considered popular, and were prepared for appropriate adult secretive and nonsecretive behavior. You had learned the tasks of growth and development well and had developed secret savvy.

15–20: Secret-keeping and secret-telling, although not major obstacles, were difficult for you. Concealing and revealing confidences with even close friends were done with some trepidation and periodic trauma. The experiences created uneasy moments in your adolescence, affected your relationships, and sent you into adulthood with anxiety about handling secrets.

0–14: You may remember a series of rejections when you were a teenager because you were either too open or too closed. Perhaps you can now realize that you suffered frequently from secrecy or disclosure strain or secrecy or disclosure shock. You may also recall that relationships with your friends and/or parents were problematic.

Having taken this quiz and read the results, you can see where the problem areas in your teenage years were. As we review the growth and development stage of adolescence, you will want to pay particular attention to the phases that pertain to those areas. Understanding why you answered as you did will give you more clues to your adult secretive or nonsecretive nature.

The Push and Pull of Being a Teenager

Although adolescence is a time when your parents are very important people, you are still shifting precariously between your need to be independent from them and your continuing dependence on them for emotional and financial support. You want to be an individual but you also want to identify with your peers and not be too dissociated from your mother and father.

This push and pull of dependence against independence creates conflicts, and they are compounded by your constantly changing physical, sexual, emotional, and intellectual self.

"Who am I?" becomes the phrase synonymous with these years,

and you are the one who is uttering it. You are trying to get a bearing on your new identity, which is so diffuse at times that it is hard to know who you really are.

These years are almost like starting life over. As you give up an identity based solely on your parents and their value system, you move on to untested and untried ground. There you must devise your own mores, goals, and sense of self.

The Clique and Intimates

One of the best ways to establish an image is to turn to an intimate group of peers. Getting in with a clique enables you to share your innermost feelings with its members. You can also start evaluating new standards for yourself within the safety of these friends and begin developing more intimate relationships with the opposite sex.

It is no wonder that a recent University of Chicago study discovered that the most popular pursuit among teens during an average day is spending time with each other. One-third of the day, in fact, passes in conversation, and 13 percent takes place on the phone.

You no doubt remember the hours you spent on the telephone. It offered you privacy, time away from your parents, and closeness with your friends. You may also recall the hours you spent alone.

The University of Chicago study also found that teenagers are by themselves 25.6 percent of the day; usually at home, and frequently in their bedrooms with the door shut.

You need all this privacy and the exclusivity with your friends to develop independence from your parents and to catch up with the changes that you are going through.

Privacy and Secrecy/Disclosure

While this self-discovery is going on, you are finding that secrecy and disclosure are playing a major role in your life. You are using them as you did in the past: to avoid punishment, to prevent rejection, to heal a past trauma, and to create bonds. You are also realizing that secrecy and disclosure have many new uses and that they can especially help you experiment with your evolving physical, emotional, sexual, and intellectual self.

It is in this stage of growth and development that you are to learn four new tasks: how to protect your changing image; how to treat your emerging sexuality; how to deal with your need to be accepted, and how to have a reciprocally intimate relationship with the opposite sex. The way you conceal and reveal private information in these areas and the reactions you receive help put the finishing touches on your adult secret-handling nature.

PRIVACY PROPS

To learn the secrecy/disclosure tasks of adolescence you have to spend time away from your parents and by yourself. Your mother and father have to provide a climate where you feel relatively secure about being independent and out of their presence. They achieve this by giving you what I call privacy props: access to a car, your own bedroom or special area in the house, use of the phone, and the freedom to write in a diary.

Unfortunately some parents become nervous when their teenagers turn private. Their fears often stem from their own adolescence when they were rebellious and suffered consequences. They want to protect their kids from the mistakes that they made. Sometimes they also just have trouble letting go.

One day Madelaine called while I was discussing adolescent problems during my radio show. She was in a panic after having read her daughter's diary and discovering that she was having a torrid affair with a British rock star.

When I suggested that this affair was most likely a fantasy, she agreed but said she was horrified that her daughter knew so much about sex.

Listening to a sample of Gywnn's dairy reassured me that these were healthy sexual adolescent feelings. Once again I tried to allay her mother's fears. Then I asked her how she felt about having violated her daughter's privacy.

She realized that it was wrong, she said, but she had gotten into sexual trouble as a teen and for that reason found it hard not to ride herd on Gywnn. I urged her to walk the fine line between giving her daughter the independence she needed and being aware of her activities. The best approach would be to talk with her in an unintrusive, supportive, and open manner.

After speaking with Madelaine I felt she would give Gywnn her privacy. Did your parents allow you to have yours?

If you didn't have the props necessary to learn the four tasks of secrecy and disclosure, you may find today that you have a too open or too closed nature and feel anxious whenever you have to reveal or conceal personal information.

Secrecy Experimentation

Once you have a sense of independence from your parents and you have gathered all or some of the privacy props, you begin to experiment with secrets and your changing identity. The experiences may be threatening, but if you handle each with the appropriate secrecy/disclosure choice, you will find the results satisfying.

PROTECTING A CHANGING SELF-IMAGE

Remember standing alone in front of a mirror as an adolescent, mentally comparing your body with everyone else's? There was no class where these differences were more apparent than in physical education, and no place where they were more skillfully hidden if you were not developing as fast as the other kids.

Lois wanted breasts like her good friends Arliss and Jacquie. Hers weren't even close in cup size. In fact, she hardly had any breasts at all. Lois solved her problem by secretly wearing cotton pad falsies in her bra, which increased her bust size from 32AA to 32B.

One day, while Lois was playing coed volleyball, her bra strap broke. She was at the net busy acing balls and didn't even think about stopping to fix it. Suddenly she heard giggles and then saw the girls and boys on the opposite court looking at her feet. To her horror, she understood why they were laughing . . . one of her falsies was lying on the asphalt!

Lois ran from the court and raced home. Her mother was at work and Lois found herself in an empty house, crying her eyes out. After a while the doorbell rang and Lois was embarrassed when she answered it and saw Arliss on the porch. Her friend refused to go away, and Lois soon suggested she come into the house.

Once inside, Arliss heard how upset Lois was and decided to tell her a secret. She admitted to her friend that she too wore falsies and was quite sure that several other girls on the volleyball team that day did too. "The only difference," Arliss added, "is that we sew ours into our bras."

Arliss's confession calmed Lois and made her feel extremely close to her. She also realized that Arliss had put the entire incident in perspective.

An hour later, Arliss and Lois returned to school, although this time Lois's falsies were sewn in. That afternoon Lois saw her friends as well as some of the boys and girls from her gym class, but nobody mentioned the episode, not that day nor in the days or weeks to come. Lois's friend had been right. Her classmates identified with her, each in his or her own way, and in deciding not to bring up Lois's secret perhaps each kept their own more secure.

If you had an embarrassing experience with your body as a teenager and a secret played a role in it, you could still be feeling the effects today.

Should you have been like Lois and met with acceptance, you are probably able to discuss with humor and ease certain personal physical characteristics that aren't movie-star gorgeous. If, however, you had a bad time of it, you may be unreasonably closed about your body as an adult so that you can avoid any type of embarrassment. Or you could be extremely open so that you get the first laugh.

EMERGING SEXUALITY

Learning to handle lust in adolescence is very important. It isn't easy because you are confused and conflicted by what your parents say, what your friends expect, and how your body feels.

Making love initially can be either a positive or unsettling experience. The way you use secrecy or disclosure with this "first time" can be as influential to your future dealings with sex as the act itself.

Nick came to me because he was unable to maintain an erection. Since he planned to marry in a few months, he was alarmed and wanted help. As we talked, Nick said he desired sex but found he had to have a few drinks to get him going. Then, once he got going, he couldn't keep going.

I asked Nick about his first sexual experience. Shifting in the chair, he admitted that it wasn't good. When he was seventeen, his buddies took him to a prostitute to lose his virginity. He was so scared that he got so drunk he couldn't perform. Nick never told his friends about what had really happened, but rather boasted of his prowess.

Hearing about that episode, I suggested to Nick that his dysfunction might be both physical and emotional. The liquor had probaby affected his initial performance (too much alcohol sometimes does cause impotence). From that point on, he had expected mistakenly that he would always have those problems. I recommended that he stop drinking before sex and put the past behind him.

Later, Nick telephoned to tell me that sex with his wife was getting much better. He had followed my directions and was conquering his fears.

Sex is a private act, but when you are a teenager it is important to talk with a close friend about the experience or your feelings of lust. From those conversations you can gain perspective on yourself and sex.

If as a teenager you had a confidant with whom you shared your sexual thoughts and experiences, you may find as an adult that you can discuss sex comfortably with your lover or spouse. Should you not have been able to talk about your experimentation, you could be an adult whose present sexual behavior is still being influenced by an adolescent sexual secret. You may be closed about your sexuality because you rarely discussed it or you could be too open because you never had the chance to discuss it and are overcompensating so that people don't think you are naive.

THE NEED FOR ACCEPTANCE

Teenagers are often pushed into being smart and successful. When something happens that indicates that they are not as bright as they should be, they can become frightened and secretive.

When Brigitte entered a new high school, she was asked to take an IQ test even though she was a strong B+ student. Later she and her mother met with the scholastic counselor, who went over her grades and glanced at the IQ results. He then proceeded to tell Brigitte's mother that Brigitte could take plane geometry and other advanced math classes but the mother would have to sign a paper saying that her daughter could not be expected to achieve more than a passing grade.

Brigitte was embarrassed and, as her mother signed the form, Brigitte caught sight of her IQ score. It was 100. Brigitte was aghast. She knew that her score was just average.

Frightened that others would discover the results of the test, Brigitte kept the score a secret and mercilessly drove herself academically, eventually graduating with honors and a partial scholarship to the state university.

At college, Brigitte studied long and hard and was rewarded with dean's list recognition. Then one day after Brigitte received a mid-term A in psychology I, the professor began discussing IQ tests and asked everybody to take one. Brigitte was anxious, but she went along with the assignment. Within a week she was given her score. It was 110.

During the lecture, the professor explained how IQ rankings usually vary by about no more than five or ten points each time a person is tested. Brigitte, once again feeling inferior, decided to talk with him after class. She was beginning to suffer signs of strain from the pressure she was putting on herself.

Brigitte's professor listened to her story and reassured her. She wasn't dumb, he said; she was probably test-phobic. He explained how smart people often have trouble with standardized tests because they try so hard to do well. He felt she was a very intelligent young woman.

Brigitte fought back the tears. She was so relieved she didn't have to continue to fight against those odds she had felt in the past. Soon she became relaxed and open about herself. She began enjoying the social side of college as well as the academic. Brigitte realized that being closed about her scholastic fears had prevented her from gaining a perspective on her abilities in high school and receiving realistic feedback from her friends and teachers.

Learning to share your fears with the appropriate people can help you deal with your teenage concerns and prevent those fears from becoming possible phobias or neurotic beliefs. Revealing secrets with peers whom you trust helps you and them develop a sense of confidence, a feeling of acceptance, and a balanced secrecy/disclosure nature.

INTIMACY WITH THE OPPOSITE SEX

One of the most important experiences you can have as a teenager is a reciprocally intimate relationship with a member of the opposite sex. This special involvement teaches you the benefits of true intimacy. By being appropriately open with another person and sharing your secrets, you see yourself in a loving, valuable, accepting and trusting light.

Bliss was a freshman in college, majoring in political science and so involved in her studies that she rarely dated. She also had a secret dream that she wanted to share with someone, but she knew she would have to find just the right man. Bliss had always wanted to be President of the United States, but she stopped telling that to people, even her family, because everyone laughed at her.

When Bliss joined the debate team she met Raymond and found that they had many things in common. Both were ambitious and wanted to change the world. Raymond hoped to end world hunger, a most impressive dream and one that Bliss and anyone could easily understand and praise. The moment Raymond asked her if she had any special aspiration, Bliss closed up. Her behavior surprised him, and he pressed to know why she had become so secretive.

After several minutes of lame excuses, Bliss finally told Raymond that she wanted to be President. She awaited his laughter. His reaction delighted her. Raymond thought it was a great idea and said he would look forward to presenting his hunger program to her at the White House.

By sharing a special side of herself, Bliss felt accepted. She and Raymond continued to deepen their relationship by revealing their innermost secrets to one another. Soon they were in love and inseparable.

If your experience with a member of the opposite sex was reciprocally intimate during your teenage years you are more likely to become an adult with a true capacity for intimacy. If there were problems or if you had no one at all, you may have missed the opportunity to practice secret-reciprocity. Today you may be having a difficult time maintaining relationships because you are unable to respond appropriately when someone shares a secret with you. You may find that you are either too open or too closed with your reply.

GROWING ONWARD

As an adolescent you were learning to be open with your peers, to keep secrets from your parents, and to be intimate with one person of the opposite sex. By concealing and revealing information so you could experiment with your changing self-image, emerging sexuality, need for acceptance, and a reciprocally intimate relationship, you were developing your adult personality and your secrecy/disclosure nature.

If your experiences were positive and the tasks that you had previously learned were still serving you in good stead, you were ready to leave this stage with secret savvy.

Should these years have been problematic and the stages before them troublesome, then you would be entering adulthood lacking in secrecy/disclosure skills.

PART THREE

Secrecy/Disclosure in Adulthood

By having identified the many factors that influenced your adult too open or too closed nature you can now understand why you find yourself operating in your Interpersonal Secrecy/Disclosure Universe and ranking as you do on the Secrecy/Disclosure Scale.

Since you are striving for a more balanced secret-keeping and secret-telling nature, you will want to modify your too open or too closed self.

Although change won't happen automatically, I can help you learn to handle secrets, starting now. By incorporating my suggestions into your daily routine, you can select the appropriate secrecy/disclosure decision. In the process you will see how your fears about being open or closed may be unfounded. As you continue to follow my lead, you will develop secrecy/disclosure skills and, as a result, your more balanced nature will evolve.

Come with me as we look at your present-day dealings with secrecy and disclosure. By understanding how to use secrets you can begin to change your life. Your relationships will improve and your professional associations will be more satisfying.

7

Family Secrets

LILY was nine years old when her cat gave birth to five kittens. She was thrilled with her new pets and spent most of her free time playing with them.

One night Lily became so involved with the kittens that she was late for dinner. Her father was not amused, and, in a rage, he put the kittens in a burlap sack, filled the bathtub with water, and held the bag under the water until the animals drowned.

Her father forced Lily to watch this ordeal and threatened to kill the mother cat if Lily ever told anyone what had happened. She was so scared that she agreed never to talk about the incident even with her mother, who she knew had heard the entire episode from the kitchen.

As Lily grew up, the secret festered inside her. She wanted to hate her father for his cruelty and her mother for her passivity, but she felt she couldn't. Lily reasoned that she needed them both for her survival.

Instead of putting the blame where it belonged, Lily assumed the responsibility for the kittens' death. The incident convinced her that she must have been a bad child, unworthy of her father's love, for him to have done such a terrible thing.

In the years that followed, Lily tried to regain her father's acceptance. She acted the part of the perfect daughter, but the effort never seemed to work. He continued to be abusive.

When Lily entered high school, she transferred her need to be loved by her father to the boys in her class. She did many favors to win their affection, but none of the ploys worked. The boys only regarded her as peculiar. Their reaction reinforced Lily's assumption that she was unlovable.

At twenty-three, Lily became engaged. It was at this point that her mother decided it was time for a long overdue heart-to-heart conversation. Initially she apologized to her daughter for not saving those five precious kittens. When Lily asked why she had been so callous, her mother replied that she had feared for her own personal safety.

Then Lily listened to the nightmare account of her parents' marriage. She heard how her father's temper had been unleashed on her mother and caused her to go to the hospital emergency room several times. She shook her head in sadness when she realized that her mother never told anyone what was going on because she wanted everyone to think highly of her husband.

As the story continued, Lily learned that the kitten drowning experience was the turning point in her parents' relationship. Still, it took her mother five more years before she could summon up the courage to file for divorce and seek professional help.

Thinking the horror was over, Lily hugged her mother and cried. It was then she discovered that the bad times might have ended for her mother but they could be continuing for her.

Lily listened as her mother talked about seeing me in therapy. I had warned her that Lily could unknowingly be bending over backward to please men and might even take abuse from them.

A few days later, I began counseling Lily. She admitted that she had repressed many of her father's hostile acts from her memory. Then she confessed that her future husband was treating her in an abusive way.

After several sessions, Lily canceled the wedding entirely. The next year, she moved to another city. Recently she wrote to say that she was pursuing a career in accounting and was dating a man who was loving and supportive. He was nothing like her father.

SECRECY/DISCLOSURE HERITAGE

Like Lily, we all grew up in families where certain behavior was handled with secrecy and we hid specific incidents from each other or the outside world. In the growth and development chapters that you have just read, you began to identify the ways in which your mother's or father's secrecy/disclosure behavior influenced you and how you became involved in conflict cycles.

It is powerful to see through adult eyes the effect that your family had on you. Actually it is the first step toward reaching a balanced nature. Once you recognize why you tend to be too open or too closed you can start to consider the options that will enable you to change.

One of these options is clearing up the secrecy/disclosure heritage that your family left you: your too open or too closed nature and the strain created by unresolved family secrets.

Lily's case history shows how important it was for her to modify her highly impermeable self and put in perspective her secret about the kittens' drowning. If she had not, Lily probably would have married into a relationship that mirrored her parents'. She could have become a battered wife and a woman who kept her husband's violent temper a secret. This could have happened because Lily had learned to imitate her mother's closed nature and low self-esteem.

What type of secrecy/disclosure heritage did your family leave you?

Although you have determined that you have a too open or too closed approach to dealing with secrets, you will want to delve deeper into the reason. The more you know about the influences that shaped your approach, the easier it will be to modify it.

You may not be sure if a family secret has left you a legacy of secrecy strain. It is essential that you find out, because if you are living with a hidden experience, it could be affecting your emotional well-being and your relationship with your mother, father, siblings, or relatives.

Initially you may respond that your family was open and had few secrets. Or you could feel that the confidences you kept were not particularly traumatic. Before you make any decisions, you will want to answer these questions:

- What personal information did you, your parents, siblings, and relatives keep from the outside world?
- What confidences did you share with a brother or sister but not with your parents?
- What special secrets did your mother or father tell you?
- Did a secret you shared cause a rift between you and a sibling or parent? Does that split still exist?
- Did a confidence you kept cause a personality adjustment that is part of your behavior?

Your response has probably led you to realize that your family did have secrets and that you could be influenced by them today.

It is time to free yourself from past conflict cycles and from your parents' unbalanced secretive or nonsecretive nature. The option is yours once you have considered whether your family used secrets in a constructive or destructive manner, was too open or too closed, and concealed or revealed certain types of secrets.

FAMILIAL SECRETS: CONSTRUCTIVE VS. DESTRUCTIVE

A family is a special unit of people who are committed to the group's survival. Its members are bound by biological roots and/or social or cultural ties to support, love, nourish, and protect one another. Their hereditary link and generational interaction create a lifeline of personal and interpersonal information. It is that background that makes up a family's uniqueness and solidifies its connection.

Secrets complement the survival tasks of a family, because when used appropriately, they provide protection, insure privacy, enhance pride, and intensify love. They do this when they:

- prevent the outside world from intruding on a family member's right to privacy,
- shield children from knowing something that is person-

ally threatening about themselves, a parent, sibling, or relative,
- guard the privacy of a family member from others in the group,
- strengthen alliances between those family members who share a mutual confidence,
- create a sense of belonging by defining the family as a group and setting it apart from the rest of the world.

Secrets can be very constructive, but when they are misused, they can become destructive. They are a negative force when they:

- undermine family loyalty as confidences are withheld from certain members,
- work to idealize a child, parent, or relative to the detriment of the individual's mental or physical health,
- trap family members in self-destructive behavior patterns,
- punish a parent, offspring, or relative by exposing a fault to the outside world or inappropriate member of the family,
- frighten children with information that they are too young to handle,
- upset subgroup alliances because some members demand to know everything,
- break down family boundaries because secrets are shared indiscriminately with outsiders.

The mishandling of secrets obstructs a family's interpersonal growth, causes dissension, interferes with children's ability to learn how to treat secrets, and creates a crippling emotional residue that can affect family members throughout their lives.

Your family tended to deal with secrets in a generally constructive or destructive way, based on its secretive or nonsecretive nature. That pattern of behavior influenced your secrecy/disclosure skills and in the process shaped your approach to managing secrets as an adult.

In the growth and development chapters we looked at the effect your mother and father had as individuals on your too open or too closed self. Now let's consider your family's influence as a whole.

Types of Familial Secrecy/Disclosure

A family pattern is different from and more than the sum of its individual members' secretive or nonsecretive natures. For example, your family could have been a combination of highly permeable and highly impermeable selves. Depending on how those open and closed types fit together, one of three patterns emerged: fearful (too closed); unconnected (too open), or unified (balanced).

Let's look at these three family patterns so you can identify yours and learn how to modify its effect.

THE FEARFUL FAMILY

Some families perceive the world as a dangerous place. Their members feel that strangers should not be trusted.

In these families, secrets are shared within the group, but parents instruct their children never to disclose what they know to anyone else. This makes it difficult for the children, especially adolescents, to establish ties in the community and to make friends. Their normal desire to separate from their parents is discouraged because it is seen as antifamily.

There is an unspoken fear among those in this unit that the family is not very strong and could be destroyed if its imperfections were made public. Consequently, each member guards the group's image. Outsiders, including those who could be helpful with family problems, are considered a threat. By locking out physicians, mental health professionals, members of the clergy, and others, unhealthy behaviors like alcoholism or problems like mental retardation are often left to continue.

Children who are raised in such a closed environment usually become distrustful of others. They have trouble sharing secrets as adults and this limits their ability to be intimate.

If you grew up in this type of atmosphere, you can now understand even more clearly why you scored on the closed side of the Secrecy/Disclosure Scale. You can also begin to recognize why you have found sharing secrets outside your family such an uncomfortable experience. If you are married, you could be perpetuating this fearful pattern in your own family.

I would encourage you to modify your secretive behavior but do start slowly. Begin by confiding in people other than your family. At first, share secrets that are not too revealing. Then you can increase your vulnerability gradually and sense the new intimacy and trust by degrees. You will discover that your flaws are not monumental and through secret-reciprocity, you will find that no one else is perfect.

THE UNCONNECTED FAMILY

The natural desire to bond and belong is lost on the second type of family. Best described as unconnected, it has no sense of loyalty or togetherness. The members do not appear to care which personal secrets are shared with the outside world.

Children raised in this indiscriminately open way do not understand the meaning of connection. They have difficulty learning to keep confidences, find it hard to make commitments to others, and in relationships that do develop, they lack the skills that help them know when to conceal and what to reveal.

The unconnected family tends to see the world as a safe environment and those who live in it as extremely trustworthy. Its members are almost childlike in their handling of secrets because they assume that only love and acceptance will come from being honest. Unfortunately, they are often burned when a confidence that they have told comes back to haunt them. They also find it difficult to maintain friendships because they treat everyone's secrets as they do their own. Frequently they violate privileged information and hurt others unwittingly.

If you were raised in an unconnected family your tendency to rank on the open side of the Secrecy/Disclosure Scale will be more understandable to you now. You realize that you didn't learn to treat disclosure discreetly nor to feel secure about secrecy.

I suggest that you begin developing secrecy/disclosure skills that create intimacy rather than arguments. You can do that by being less impulsive with disclosure. Think before you tell. Ask yourself if the person who is hearing the secret is trustworthy and consider whether or not what you are revealing is privileged information. In general, remember you have a right to privacy and so do others.

THE UNIFIED FAMILY

Sharing secrets constructively is the hallmark of the unified family. The trust, respect, and esteem that its members accord each other breed intimacy and a value for privacy.

This family thrives on its bonding and loyalty; is basically secure and not afraid of imperfections, all of which leads its members to use secrets among themselves and the outside world in an appropriate manner. They are not fearful of being known but they are aware of when to protect their privacy and whom to trust with their most intimate confidences.

In this unit, secrets are rarely kept just to maintain the family's image if one of its members needs help. Confidences are seldom used as weapons to hurt feelings or reputations, and they are never shared with a young child until the offspring is old enough to handle them.

Adults in this kind of family do not protest if certain subgroups such as siblings share secrets among themselves. This is because the unified family members are confident in their love for one another and they recognize the value of everyone's privacy as well as their need for connections.

If you grew up within a unified pattern, you probably scored in the middle range of the Secrecy/Disclosure Scale. You tend to feel comfortable when you conceal or reveal secrets. You have satisfying relationships outside the family and treat others' secrets as you do your own.

Should you wish to enhance your abilities, I encourage you to be more aware of your instinctive techniques. Then you can intensify the benefits of secrecy and disclosure by enjoying privacy without guilt and by sharing deeper confidences.

A DIFFERENT NATURE?

You may have discovered that your family's secretive or nonsecretive nature is different from yours. Sometimes a child will rebel against a family pattern because it is uncomfortable. Growing up in a fearful family, for example, you may have decided that you did not like being a member of a closed unit. Unfortunately, without appropriate role models, the openness you hoped to achieve was not attained and as an adult you may tend to be too open.

The converse of this example would be true if you were raised in an unconnected family.

The way to modify your nature is to refer to the previously described family pattern that reflects your more or less permeable or impermeable adult "self."

THE LEGACY

By reviewing these three patterns, you have been able to determine if your family used secrecy or disclosure in a constructive or destructive manner. You have also identified the first half of your secrecy/disclosure heritage by uncovering how your family unit helped influence the shaping of your too open, too closed, or balanced self.

Since most people are raised within a fearful or unconnected pattern, your legacy is probably an unbalanced approach to managing secrets.

You have started to learn ways to modify that approach and I will help you build on those skills as we continue our secret journey. Eventually your legacy of being too open or too closed will have little effect on you because you will have developed an expertise that will enable you to handle secrecy and disclosure appropriately.

Familial Secrets

When you were with your parents, siblings, or relatives, you may have shared confidences that today are still affecting your behavior and emotional well-being. This secrecy strain, which could range from sibling animosity to deep psychological trauma, is the second half of your family's secrecy/disclosure heritage. Unless you disinherit yourself from this legacy by resolving those secrets you could live with their repercussions for the rest of your life.

To determine if you have destructive residue from past family secrets, let's consider the five different types of confidences usually at play in the home. I categorize them as Vault Material, Unmentionable Indiscretions, For Our Ears Only, Time-lapsed Data, and Familial Discretion.

VAULT MATERIAL

As a child you may have decided to keep something to yourself. You were afraid that if the confidence was shared with parents, siblings, or relatives, you would be misunderstood or rejected.

Vault material might be a harmless idiosyncrasy or some antisocial or destructive behavior. When dangerous information is concealed, the concealment stunts a person's growth, creates anxiety, and jeopardizes the family's image without its knowledge.

Harrison was a sixty-five-year-old widower, a retired businessman, and a grandfather. Everyone thought he was above reproach. Then one day that image was shattered. He was arrested for exposing himself in the park.

When Mona picked her father up at the police station, she was mortified by his behavior and panicked because a reporter had filed a story about the incident.

Once they arrived home, Mona told her husband what had happened. He thought the episode had probably been triggered by Harrison's loneliness, until his father-in-law admitted that he had always been a flasher. He told how as a child, he had seen a man expose himself several times. Harrison had been shocked and thrilled by the experience. He also had been fascinated by the power the man seemed to have over others.

At first, Harrison imitated the flasher as any child might, but soon the mimicking became a habit. In high school and college his periodic flashing was dismissed as prankster behavior, but even then he realized he had a serious problem. He just couldn't discuss it with anyone.

After he married, Harrison continued to expose himself in public. He was arrested once, but it was in another city and he was able to conceal the offense.

After hearing her father's story, Mona suggested that he see a therapist. Then she agreed to keep the recent arrest a secret. Since the rest of the family lived in other states, they probably wouldn't see the article. She felt her father had been embarrassed enough. Mona wanted to protect his privacy from other family members who might not be as understanding.

Today Harrison is no longer a flasher. Although a small story ran in the local paper, none of the relatives or close friends saw it. If they did, no one mentioned the article.

Vault material can be dangerous if it contains socially unacceptable or personally threatening material. It can lock you in a childhood conflict cycle as it locked Harrison. As an adult you could find yourself repeating your past behavior or reacting with anxiety whenever you think about what you have concealed.

UNMENTIONABLE INDISCRETIONS

You may have been involved in a secret that was shared with others in the family but never acknowledged by any of them.

Sometimes parents, children, or relatives participate in harmful familial behavior. Since the act is so menacing, each refuses to discuss it or to do anything about stopping it.

Incidents that are unmentionable indiscretions may include child or wife abuse, incest, murder, rape, and robbery. By concealing what is happening, the family allows it to continue.

Lily and her mother trapped themselves in an unmentionable indiscretion because they wanted to maintain a perfect image to each other and to the outside world. The denial of the abuse even brought Lily and her mother to rationalize that the problem was their fault.

Think back to your own family. If you or any of its members hid destructive behavior or accepted the blame for it, you still could be feeling angry toward your parents or siblings. You also could be repeating the behavior in your own home.

FOR OUR EARS ONLY

You and your family may have decided that it was important to protect the privacy of one of your own from the outside world. You could have been afraid of being stigmatized if the situation became public.

The following example illustrates how detrimental it can be to shield a family member if the secret is hazardous to the person's health.

Bella's grandmother, Gretel, came to live with the family when she was in her sixties. Gretel had always been a vital woman, but her husband's death seemed to have changed her. She began to experience extreme mood changes and forgetfulness.

When Bella told her mother how worried she was about Grandma, her fears were dismissed. She was told that elderly people do become irrational as they get older. What she wasn't told about by her mother was the family's embarrassment over Gretel's behavior and the growing fear that she was going insane.

Rather than getting Gretel help, Bella's mother kept her in the back bedroom and allowed her no visitors. Soon everyone in the family, including Bella, began to rationalize that Gretel was senile and that nothing could be done.

One day, Gretel collapsed in her room. She was rushed to the hospital. Besides a serious heart problem, she was diagnosed as having Alzheimer's disease. She died a few weeks later from a heart attack.

Bella and her family were shocked. They also were filled with guilt and grief. By protecting their image, they had allowed their grandmother to suffer without treatment or compassion. Still, none of them talked about what had happened or the role they had played in the incident. Finally, years later, Bella discussed it with her mother and shared her feelings about how it continued to haunt her. Then the family sat down and talked about what had happened. Once they admitted their mistake, they were able to lessen the anxiety and guilt that they were experiencing.

If you were a party to disguising a family member's mental or physical condition, perhaps even your own, you will have many reactions to that secret in adulthood. Should the person still be alive or if you continue to have the problem, neither of you may be getting the help you need.

TIME-LAPSED DATA

You may remember being told certain family secrets after you had reached a particular age. Your parents or relatives said you were ready to hear something important about yourself or someone else. They took you into their confidence and, with that gesture, a stronger familial alliance was forged.

As a child, you needed to be exposed slowly to family secrets and to be protected from secretive collusions as well as adult confidences that you were too young to handle.

Kit, at thirty-five, was still reeling from a secret his mother had shared with him and his brother, Max. The side effects for Kit had been anxiety, sibling animosity, and fear for his mental stability.

When Kit was ten, his mother told him and his twelve-year-old brother that she was having an affair with their father's employer. She swore both boys to secrecy. Kit was shocked by his mother's confession. He felt guilty about keeping it from his father, but decided that he had no alternative. As a result, Kit found himself distanced from the man he loved because he was afraid a slip of the tongue might expose his mother and cause a divorce.

Max reacted differently. He had always put his mother on a pedestal. When she told him the secret, he refused to believe it. He never mentioned the illicit romance to anyone. Max's reaction soon caused a rift between the two boys.

Twenty-five years later, Kit contacted me. He related how he had talked to his brother and that Max continued to maintain that his mother had never been unfaithful. Max's perception disturbed him greatly.

Kit wondered if he was losing his mind. He began to think that perhaps he did make it all up about his mother's indiscretion. If he had, Kit said, then he had ruined a relationship with his father for no reason and created an estrangement between his brother and himself needlessly.

I suggested that Kit ask his mother to clarify the episode. Once he knew for certain what had happened, maybe then he would be able to drop the subject and even let Max have his denial.

Kit's mother verified the affair. Her admission made him feel better about his soundness of mind. It allowed him to let Max off the hook and enabled the brothers to mend the rift that had existed for twenty-five years.

This case history shows how destructive it can be to share an adult secret with a young child. Kit was unable to deal with the content of the secret and its concealment. As a result he experienced years of distress. His mother never should have burdened him or Max with her extramarital liaison. Unfortunately parents often use their children to keep secrets from each other. It is a hostile statement toward a mate and designed to split a child's allegiance.

If you were made privy to incidents that frightened you as a child you probably had many reactions. Unless those episodes and feelings were resolved, they could be causing you emotional and interpersonal problems today.

FAMILIAL DISCRETION

Although your family had some secrets that were to remain within the group, there were others that you could share with outsiders. You probably remember being told that you might tell a close friend a confidence, but you should do so discreetly and only if the individual was trustworthy.

Familial secrets that were disclosed to outsiders enabled you to gain perspective on yourself, your parents, siblings, and relatives. They also let you discover how confidences can create intimacy and stimulate reciprocity.

If your family shared confidential information indiscriminately with the outside world, you may have decided that you could not tell any of its members about your private life. Since they tended to be too open, you became closed toward them and may be distrustful of them to this day.

For example, Shelley lived in a house where secrets were revealed impulsively to outsiders. The whole town always knew the family's personal business.

When Shelley decided to have an abortion, she wanted to go through it with her mother and sisters, but she couldn't risk telling them because they would make it public knowledge. Although Shelley wasn't ashamed of her decision, she felt that she should have the right to choose who would know.

Today Shelley's abortion is still a secret from her family, and so are many other aspects of her life, which she would like to share.

Should your family have treated you as Shelley's treated her, you may have had personal information disclosed to the wrong people and found yourself exposed in ways that upset you. As an adult, you could be mad at your family for what it has done and sorry that you cannot enjoy the type of intimacy with its members that you would like.

A HEALTHY APPROACH TO FAMILY SECRETS

You may have recalled one or more family secrets after considering the five basic types found in most homes: Vault Material, Unmentionable Indiscretions, For Our Ears Only, Time-lapsed Data, and Familial Discretion.

The time has come to disinherit yourself from the secrecy strain that these secrets may be causing you. You can achieve your goal by taking three steps: (1) defining the confidence, (2) discussing the incident, and (3) resolving the experience.

As you take each step, do it carefully and proceed slowly. Reevaluate as you continue and ask yourself if the action that you have chosen seems right. Always remember that a family therapist may be useful, especially if you stumble into an area that feels as if it is over your head. A single consultation may be all you need to clear things up.

Once you complete this process, your emotional well-being will improve and you will be able to rebuild the familial relationships that have been affected in a negative way.

STEP 1. DEFINING THE CONFIDENCE

Although you may remember some aspects of the secret, you will want to recall as much as possible. The more you can remember, the easier it will be to deal with the experience.

Take a piece of paper and a pencil and write down the following:

- the incident that was concealed, the person or people involved, the consequences, and your childhood reactions,
- how you feel the secret has influenced your present relationship with different family members,
- what you sense are the emotional side effects caused by your secretive behavior.

Having written about the situation, you may have started to see it in a different perspective. As you release any secret from deep inside yourself, you begin to desensitize the confidence's effect on you. At the moment you may be feeling less anxious about the experience and more secure about revealing it.

When you find that you have recalled as much of what happened as possible, you are ready to move on to the next phase of freeing yourself from your secrecy strain.

STEP 2. DISCUSSING THE INCIDENT

You will want to consider the most appropriate and comfortable way for you to disclose your secret. I suggest you select one of the following:

- an audio-cassette recorder so you can tape your disclosure and hear it played back to you;
- a family member who was involved in the situation, but who would not be threatened by discussing the episode and your feelings;
- an uninvolved member of the family, who would lend insight into the incident;
- a nonjudgmental, uninvolved third party, who will honor the confidentiality of your disclosure and be able to help you understand what happened and your reactions;
- a mental health professional, who can explore the layers of feelings that you have and help you analyze the more severe repercussions.

Hearing the secret played back or being told will release more anxiety surrounding the incident and will help you gain additional insight into what occurred. By continuing to deal with your secret, you are defusing its power over you. You are also dealing with the nonverbal logic "I am hiding something bad about me; therefore I am bad," which has encouraged you to keep your secret. You now realize there were many factors involved in the concealment of this situation. Several, or maybe most, of them had nothing to do with you.

Once you have revealed your secret, you can take the final step toward ending its negative side effects.

STEP 3. RESOLVING THE EXPERIENCE

After your disclosure you have many alternatives to consider. I encourage you to select one of four directions to resolve the secret:

1. Accept what happened and put it to rest. Realize that the other participants could be threatened by discussing the episode with you. You may be able to modify your behavior, but they may not. Since the secret no longer harms you or affects them, you can leave it in the past.

2. Talk with everyone who was touched by the concealment. Together you may be able to release anxiety and be at one with each other again.

3. Discuss the confidence with a family member who never heard the secret but with whom you wish to strike up an alliance. Your disclosure could deepen your feelings for one another and encourage mutual empathy.

4. Suggest that a member of the family seek professional or medical advice. Mention that keeping the condition or the destructive behavior a secret is dangerous to his or her health as well as that of others who may have been involved in the concealment.

Having resolved your secret, you will find that you are feeling differently about certain matters and that your relationship with the family members who were involved with the confidence has changed.

Each time you take a past concealment through these three steps you will benefit. Although the process may be anxiety-provoking, you will discover that the result is more than satisfying. You will have freed yourself from a past family secret and the heritage of secrecy strain that it has left you.

A NEW LEGACY

You now have the tools and knowledge to change your secrecy/disclosure heritage. By starting to modify your unbalanced secretive or nonsecretive nature and by resolving your family secrets, you can create a new legacy for yourself. You can also feel more comfortable with your family and be free of any related guilt.

Not long ago, I was telling a friend, Trent, about researching this chapter. He told me that thirty years had passed since he ran his brother's car into the family station wagon. He never told anyone, including his parents, who continued to blame his brother for the accident. Trent admitted that he had felt guilty ever since.

As we continued to talk, he said, "This is ridiculous. I'm going to tell everyone what really happened. There is no reason to keep it a secret anymore."

8

Does Love Mean Telling All?

I keep my father's ashes in the living room but I can't tell my third husband the reason.

I had an affair with my father. It lasted 15 years. I don't really know how it started, but I do remember that one night I was having trouble sleeping and my father said that I could get in bed with him. I was about 15. My mother, his wife, had died six months earlier and we both missed her very much. We found ourselves sharing our grief and loneliness and those feelings created a special bond between us.

From that night on, I rarely slept anywhere but in my father's bed. After a time, we began to sleep in each other's arms. Then one night our hugs turned to caressing and then sex.

After I married, I continued to see my father and everything was fine until my husband caught us making love one afternoon. He divorced me soon afterwards and demanded custody of our two children. I couldn't contest the case, because my husband threatened to expose my affair.

A few years later, I remarried. Within four months, my second husband was killed in a hunting accident. My father consoled me and continued to be my best friend and lover.

Just when I thought I would never marry again, I met Ron. He was so wonderful. Even my father liked him. The night before our wedding, Ron went to a bachelor party and I went to my father. We made love passionately because I think we both realized we couldn't continue our affair. His wife was becoming suspicious and I didn't want to harm what I could have with Ron.

My father died four months ago. I miss him terribly. I asked his wife if I could have him cremated and his remains placed in a box near his photograph in my living room. I was so pleased when she agreed and so thankful that neither she nor Ron asked why. I couldn't have told either of them the truth.

I have wanted to share this long-kept secret for years. Living with it has been very difficult. Thank you for the opportunity to reveal what I did.

Signed,

AN ANONYMOUS DAUGHTER

How do you feel about this woman's decision to keep her affair from her husband and everyone else?

You probably have conflicting reactions. In relationships we are often unsure about what we should tell our spouse or lover. In some instances, we think honesty is the best policy, but in other cases, we are not so sure.

If you have ever had to make a choice regarding whether or not to reveal a secret to a loved one, you know how difficult that decision can be especially if the disclosure will put your relationship in jeopardy.

I wish I could have responded to this woman's letter. However, there was no return address on the envelope. I would have told her that she was enmeshed in a secrecy/disclosure pattern in which one person conceals the past for fear it will destroy the present relationship. I call this pattern "Previous Indiscretions."

I would have urged her to deal with the secret with a mental health professional. Just because the incest was over didn't mean it was not interfering with her marriage.

The effects of incest do not end when the sex stops. The repercussions continue until the victim is able to sort out all the feelings surrounding the incident. What the anonymous letter writer didn't realize was that her affection toward her third husband was being influenced by her secret.

Only through counseling could she understand her father's seduction. She would see how the distorted relationship with her father could be damaging her present marriage. Once she had uncovered all the emotions involved, she would be able to make a clear secrecy/disclosure decision. Her choice would not be based on fear of rejection or on guilt or shame. Instead, it would reflect a healthy need for privacy or a desire to let her her husband know her better.

MAKING SECRECY WORK

You too can learn to use secrecy and disclosure in an effective manner with your spouse or lover. Unlike the anonymous letter writer, I doubt you will need therapy. Her situation was most unusual. What you must understand is the purpose of secrecy and disclosure in relationships, the problems of being too open or too closed, the different stages of a romantic relationship, and the secrecy/disclosure pattern that is unique to each phase. Once you have this knowledge you will add to your secrecy skills and take another important step toward creating a more balanced secret-handling nature.

The Purpose and Problems of Secrecy/Disclosure

Secrets are necessary for intimacy. When they are shared in the right way, they enhance feelings by creating bonds and mutual insight. When concealed for healthy reasons, they protect privacy so you can maintain a sense of self even though you are involved with another person.

Problems arise in romantic relationships when secrets are mishandled. There are four reasons why this can happen:

- You disclose information to your mate that should be left unsaid.
- You keep your partner inappropriately in the dark about something.
- You are unaware of the negative potential effect of a secret on the relationship.

- You make your spouse or lover uncomfortable by sharing too many or too few confidences.

By mismanaging your secrets you build walls between you and your mate instead of opening doors to deeper intimacy.

You can now see how secrecy and disclosure contribute to the success or failure of an interpersonal bond.

RELATIONSHIP STAGES and SECRECY/DISCLOSURE PATTERNS

When you meet someone special, you begin using secrets immediately as you decide what your potential partner should know. If he or she finds out too much, you fear you may be rejected. On the other hand, just enough of the right information could make you appear highly desirable.

The decision to reveal or conceal continues to be a dilemma as you become more involved. Each of the three stages of a romantic relationship — idealization, realization, and commitment — elicits different feelings about being known.

In the idealization stage you want to put your best foot forward.

In the realization stage you wish to be more honest, but since you are still worried about being accepted, you hold back.

In the commitment stage you are most open, but at the same time you continue to wonder how much of your privacy should be guarded.

Ideally, every stage stimulates you to release an appropriate amount of new personal information. In that way, you get to know your beloved slowly while you gradually increase your vulnerability. Otherwise you may divulge too much too soon and leave yourself feeling naked should the relationship end without a commitment.

If you know *what to tell when,* you can prevent secrets from causing problems in your romantic relationship. To do that, you need to be aware of a series of secrecy/disclosure patterns, the types of revelations and concealment choices that recur under certain circumstances during each stage of a romantic relationship.

Whether you are looking, involved, married, or living with someone, secrecy/disclosure patterns are a powerful tool that enables you to build toward more interpersonal fulfillment. These patterns do this primarily by guiding you in appropriate disclosure and withholding behavior. They also indicate how your mate may be managing his or her secrets, pinpoint difficulties in your relationship, and let you know if you have selected Mr. or Ms. "Right."

Now that you understand the purpose of secrecy and disclosure in a romantic relationship, the problems that being too open or too closed can cause, the three stages of intimacy, and the concept of secrecy/disclosure patterns, let's consider ways to treat secrets appropriately in idealization, realization, and commitment.

The Idealization Stage and Its Secrecy/Disclosure Patterns

There is nothing like the natural high of being in love. You feel heady. You feel as if you are flying. An invisible love buffer zone seems to encircle you both and allows only positive information to pass in and out. The result is that your newly beloved seems perfectly suited for your every need and you appear to be the answer to his or her dreams. Scientists now think that this love "high" may be created by the secretion of the neurotransmitter phenylethylamine, which is chemically similar to amphetamine.

The feeling that you are made for each other is an essential part of idealization. It adds to the thrill of the initial meetings. It also tends to increase the intense feelings that will be called upon later to soften the inevitable disappointment when the other person becomes better known.

During this stage, you and your lover filter each other's behavior through the buffer zone of love as well as rose-colored glasses. In addition, you help out by putting forward your most favorable secrets and keeping the threatening ones under wraps. Should one of you, in this first stage, disclose a confidence that hints at an imperfection, the other will tend to look only for the good in the revelation rather than seeing the vital insight it may give into the loved one's character.

Let's explore the secrecy/disclosure patterns of this stage: Hidden Past, Positive Pointers, Misinterpreted Confessions, and The Risk Test. Understanding them can prevent you from being too open or

too closed, determine compatibility, and indicate mutual acceptance.

HIDDEN PAST

Since new lovers always want to put their best feet forward, they
don't usually disclose anything that will position them in a bad
light. They rarely tell negative secrets.

A Hidden Past pattern does protect you from exposing parts of
your life that you are not ready to reveal. In some instances this
protection is harmless, but sometimes it can lay the foundation for
trouble.

Basically, the decision about whether or not to conceal a secret
depends on its content. If what you are hiding could affect the very
fiber of the relationship, it is best to open up. If, on the other hand,
the secret has no bearing on the day-to-day functioning of the relationship, you may want to hold off until later, or you could decide
never to tell.

You may, for example, have flunked second grade. The experience was traumatic and even now causes you embarrassment. Since
the incident doesn't create problems in the present, it is not necessary to discuss it at this stage. You can wait until you feel more certain of your lover's acceptance.

Sometimes, however, it is important to impart a negative revelation during the idealization stage. As the following case history
shows, doing it may prevent problems later on.

Gary had a rubber fetish. Since he had been a teenager, the smell
and touch of similar materials excited him so much that when he
moved among women in vinyl raincoats, he was almost orgasmic.

When Gary fell in love with Julie, he wrote me a letter. He explained that she knew nothing of his idiosyncratic bent. He was
afraid that if she ever found out, she would consider him a pervert
and end the relationship.

I urged Gary to tell her the truth. If she found out later, I said, it
would be even more upsetting to her. I then mentioned that some
men do have rubber fetishes and their wives are often understanding if the matter is honestly discussed.

Gary did level with Julie and, although surprised, she was accepting. She decided to buy a vinyl slicker. She told Gary that if he
was going to be attracted to any woman, she wanted it to be her.

By discussing his fetish, Gary had strengthened his relationship with Julie. He had also averted a potential conflict in the future.

When you use this secrecy/disclosure pattern, don't let it cover up behavior that could affect your attachment. Instead, let it protect a confidence that has no bearing on your bond and could be told at a later date when you feel assured of your mate's support.

POSITIVE POINTERS

While you are guarding the secrets that show you to be less than perfect, you are telling ones that show off your good points. Of course, your new love is doing the same.

Positive disclosure reinforces the mutual assumption that you are 100 percent compatible. It also encourages you both to continue the courtship.

Remember Brigitte, who as a teenager thought she had an abnormally low IQ and then discovered that she was only test-phobic? In college she met Lionel, and they fell in love. He soon let her know that her intelligence was one of the reasons he had been attracted to her.

Brigitte appreciated the way Lionel gave her the benefit of the doubt. She then told him about how her high school counselor had labeled her as academically deficient.

After hearing the story, Lionel had two reactions. He sympathized with her experience and admired her for rising above what she thought might be her limits.

Lionel's empathy convinced Brigitte that he was perfect for her. He had liked what the secret said about her. It proved to him that he had found a woman who was not only smart but also able to overcome personal problems.

Brigitte's disclosure had intensified their mutual love.

The Positive Pointers pattern can be most beneficial. It enables you to show your best side and thereby stimulate the other person's love. It can help you see how supportive and understanding your potential partner can be. It is a pattern you should use often in the idealization phase.

MISINTERPRETED CONFESSIONS

If one of you disappoints the other in this stage by breaking a promise or not living up to expectations in some other way, that person may try to cover up the mistake and avoid a possible rejection by revealing a secret. Feeling complimented by being given this private information, the previously disappointed person fails to understand fully what the secret is saying about his or her beloved. He or she only feels gratified that the other person cares enough to share the confidence.

This pattern was dramatically played out by one of my clients. Terri had known George for what she described as an idyllic two months. Then, without warning, he began to stand her up. One particular evening, after he had kept her waiting for hours, she demanded an explanation.

George agreed that she deserved to know why he had been late so many times. He told her that it was because of an important secret he had to keep from everyone.

Since he loved her, however, he would share it with her. Terri immediately felt more connected to George. She then listened as he explained that he had gambling debts. Recently the men who loaned him the money had demanded that he pay up. When he refused, they started making death threats toward his ex-wife and their children.

George said that that was why he needed to be away from Terri periodically and why he appreciated the respite she offered him from the hostile world.

Terri basked in George's confession. It made her feel loved and trusted. She paid no attention to the content of the secret and what it said about George's personality and life-style. She had stepped into a dangerous relationship, but all she sensed was the warmth and safety of a person who cared enough about her to share a secret. Fortunately, therapy helped her to reevaluate the revelation and eventually find a more suitable partner.

Thinking about the Misinterpreted Confessions pattern cautions you against being swept off your feet by secret disclosures. Consider the information these confidences give you and ask yourself some candid questions about what you have heard. The answers will help you decide if you wish to pursue the relationship. Don't make Terri's mistake when you hear a secret. Listen carefully to what you are being told.

THE RISK TEST

There comes a point in the idealization stage when you decide that it is time either to move the relationship to a more intense level or break it off.

Your decision can be based on a gut reaction, the information you have gathered, or an isolated incident between you two. These observations can be valid, but there is a more reliable method.

By using the fourth pattern of this phase, the Risk Test, you can realistically judge your potential partner's suitability. You can discover how accepting of your imperfections he or she really is and how intimately compatible you are.

The Risk Test encourages you to reveal a less than positive side of yourself. The moment you are frank with your lover, you stimulate a response. It is that reaction that assists you in cutting through the superficial material that you have focused on so far. Then you can really tell if he or she is right for you.

Eileen found that the results of the Risk Test helped her decide about her future with Marshall. After dating him for four weeks, Eileen told him she was attracted to him sexually but couldn't respond to his overtures because she had herpes. She felt she couldn't go on seeing Marshall unless he knew the facts.

Marshall was surprised by Eileen's admission, but he replied that the fear of herpes wouldn't stop him from loving her or wanting to be with her sexually. He added that he was pleased she thought enough of him to reveal this personally threatening secret.

Then Marshall said that he also had a secret to share. He explained that he was not only divorced but the father of a four-year-old son. He said that he hadn't wanted to mention Jeff because he felt that Eileen might not be interested in a man with a child.

Eileen was thrilled to hear about Jeff. She was glad Marshall had been honest and asked if she could meet his son.

Marshall and Eileen were soon hugging each other in relief and with a new sense of intimacy. By risking rejection, Eileen discovered that Marshall accepted her past. She also saw how her disclosure encouraged him to share in kind. This second revelation was very important. It signaled that Marshall automatically became involved in secret reciprocity, an essential factor in determining if a couple's secrecy/disclosure natures are intimately compatible.

Partners need to be alike in their secret-keeping and secret-telling behavior. Otherwise there will be disharmony in the relationship because one divulges too much and the other too little. The mate who is more closed will feel pressured to open up and the partner who is open will feel denied true access into the other's world. It is almost impossible to achieve mutual intimacy under these circumstances.

Initially, you can utilize the Risk Test to determine whether you and your mate share a similar secretive or nonsecretive nature. I would also recommend that each of you take the Secrecy/Disclosure Scale Quiz in chapter 3. When you compare your rankings, you can identify how alike you truly are: the more alike, the better. Should you find that you are both too open or too closed, you can work together toward becoming secret savvy pros.

If the results show that you are very different, you will need to decide which of you has the more balanced nature and then move in that direction. The alternative would be to end the relationship. Although this last suggestion may sound radical, it may be best to break off with someone at this stage. You will avoid undue stress and eventual disappointment.

The four patterns of the idealization stage — Hidden Past, Positive Pointers, Misinterpreted Confessions, and The Risk Test — can help you achieve three important goals. They can (1) protect much of your privacy while you gather information about your new love, (2) enable you to risk something from your past to uncover how accepting your potential mate may be, and (3) let you discover if you and your new love have compatible secrecy/disclosure natures.

To make certain that these patterns work for your benefit, keep the following tips in mind:

1. DO tell secrets about yourself that may affect the future of the relationship, such as those dealing with sex, a past criminal record, or an addiction. As you are disclosing, notice the other person's reaction. Is it one of acceptance or rejection?

2. DO make an attempt to "hear" what your potential partner's secrets are saying about his or her character.

3. DO make sure that, as you reveal a confidence, your new love is replying in kind. If there is no reciprocity, it may be a good indication that the relationship is going nowhere and that your future mate has a problem with intimacy.

4. DO remember that you are not getting a true picture of the other person because, like you, he or she is putting the best image forward.

5. DON'T tell all your deepest and darkest secrets at the beginning of this stage. You don't know how this individual will react to keeping your confidences. By using caution now, you will not be left feeling vulnerable, exposed, and hurt should the relationship suddenly end.

Let the idealization secrecy/disclosure patterns assist you in dealing with this stage's love buffer zone and rose-colored glasses. You will enjoy the phase more and make a smoother transition to the next level of intimacy id that is your wish.

The Realization Stage and Its Secrecy/Disclosure Patterns

When the blinders come off, you start seeing one another more realistically. This candid vision is inspired by your continuing mutual desire for love, respect, and trust.

Your wish to be accepted during this stage encourages you to relate to one another on a more intimate level. You know you cannot be totally loved unless you are more fully known, so you take the risk and share the less-than-perfect side of yourself.

As each of you discovers personality flaws in the other, the facades that you both created in the idealization stage begin to crumble. Now each of you must accept that all your needs will never be met by the other person.

When you begin to see how revealing negative secrets can cause conflict, you start to wonder just how much to tell each other. You think that because you are in love, you should be able to be open about everything, but soon you are having second thoughts.

The easiest way out of this dilemma is to understand and use the four secrecy/disclosure patterns of this stage. They take the guesswork out of what you should or should not reveal. The categories are the Second Time Around, the Blame Game, the Secret Life, and To Tell or Not to Tell.

THE SECOND TIME AROUND

A secret can have many layers. In the idealization stage, you tend to expose the level that is most positive. During the realization phase, it is wise to go back to those confidences that you told previously and to elaborate on them, particularly if there is still some hidden negative aspect of the secret that was left untold.

When Brigitte, for example, disclosed to Lionel about overcoming her attitude toward a low IQ, she never mentioned that math was still an enigma to her. Without this important piece of information, Lionel assumed that she could take care of most things in their relationship. He decided to turn over the finances to her after they began living together.

The inevitable happened. When Lionel returned from a research trip, he found bounced checks and the checkbook in disarray. Brigitte admitted that she had omitted mention of her math phobia. He was angry at first but then understood that she had kept her inadequacy a secret only because she didn't want to disappoint him. He asked her to be more honest in the future, especially when it affected their life together. Lionel then agreed to handle their money matters.

Brigitte was pleased that her secret had been completely disclosed. She had seen how the Second Time Around pattern could cause problems but create bonds as well.

In this phase, it is essential to rethink what you have revealed in the past. If you left something unsaid, now may be the time to open up. You do not need to appear as perfect as you did in the idealization period.

THE BLAME GAME

If your realization stage seems headed for commitment, you do as much as possible to keep it moving in that direction. If, however, it veers off course, you may try to figure out why by doing an investigation on your own. At this point, it is important to be careful not to blame the other person too quickly for causing the difficulties when you may be the one responsible.

Rebecca had been using this pattern to her detriment for years when she wrote me a troubled letter. In it, she related a secret that she felt was destroying her present relationship.

The sight of battling women had turned Rebecca on ever since she could remember. Visualizing two females fighting enabled her to reach orgasm whether she was masturbating or having sex with a man.

This fantasy was, in fact, the only way she could find sexual satisfaction. She had come to the conclusion that the men she had known were not good lovers and that was why she needed to visualize the women. If the men were stimulating enough, she reasoned, why would she need this fantasy? She was certainly no lesbian. She had been married and had a four-year-old son.

I wrote Rebecca and suggested that she look closely at why she was blaming her sexual partners for her need to use her secret fantasy. Perhaps she had a problem of letting go with the opposite sex, and by using a fantasy, she could remain in control of her body and her pleasure. I encouraged Rebecca to see a therapist. Otherwise she would probably continue to repeat the cycle — become close to a man, find him unable to arouse her sexually, use her fantasy to achieve orgasm, and then blame the problem on the man.

Rebecca took my advice. Since then she has begun to feel less threatened by men both in and out of bed.

If you discover during the realization phase that you are accusing your mate of causing a problem, do some soul-searching. Maybe the key lies with you. Discussing the situation with a third party could clear up the dilemma, increase intimacy, and give you insight into your personality.

THE SECRET LIFE

The third secrecy/disclosure pattern involves a situation where one of you lives a hidden existence.

This type of secret is quite common, particularly in a long-drawn-out realization stage. The pattern happens because one person in the relationship allows the other to be evasive about certain not-so-private matters.

Cathleen, for example, had been dating Drew for three years but she had never been to his apartment or met his friends. He kept promising to introduce her to his buddies and show her his place, but he always found an excuse to cancel those plans.

Eventually Cathleen became suspicious and pressed to know why he was excluding her from his life. Drew finally admitted that he was living with his mother. She was very ill, he said, and couldn't stand to have people around.

Cathleen decided to check Drew's story. One day while he was at work, she called his home. A young woman answered. Cathleen hung up immediately. That night she confronted Drew, who told her she had spoken to his mother's nurse. Cathleen refused to believe him and, in the face of her mounting hysteria, he broke down and confessed that he was married. Cathleen had talked with his wife.

It was a terrible shock for her, but Cathleen was glad she had followed her instincts and finally smoked out the secret.

If you are involved with a person who is secretive about his or her life, you had better start asking questions. The confrontation might be painful, but it could prevent you from losing years of your life in a relationship that can never reach the commitment stage.

TO TELL OR NOT TO TELL

Being in love doesn't mean that you must forfeit your individuality. Healthy coupling lets you maintain a sense of self while you are also involved with another person. This means that you have a right to privacy. So does your partner.

It is natural, in the realization phase, to wonder if you should expose all your private thoughts and experiences. This dilemma causes anxiety because there are past incidents that you would probably prefer to keep under wraps. You are concerned that your mate now may have the right to know about them.

I believe that if an experience in your past has little impact on your present, there is no need for disclosure. Should you decide that you must speak up, tell only the pertinent facts and leave nonessential details to history.

Barney did precisely that. In previous relationships he had been impotent. With Roz there was no problem, and at first he decided not to reveal his past dysfunction. I suggested that he should tell Roz because it might return and Roz could be confused and blame herself. If she were prepared for the possibility, she would be more likely to be understanding and helpful.

Although I encouraged him to tell, I cautioned him that it wasn't necessary for him to discuss how the problem had influenced his previous affairs and how those lovers had dealt with it. In this way, Barney could be honest with Roz but still maintain a sense of privacy.

Never feel guilty about wanting to keep certain personal facts to yourself. If you are unsure about an untold secret's effect on you or your lover, discuss it in confidence with a nonjudgmental third party. A member of the clergy, a therapist or a good friend should be able to give you some perspective. Then your decision about concealing or revealing will be easier to make.

By using these four patterns — the Second Time Around, the Blame Game, the Secret Life, and To Tell or Not To Tell — you can (1) gain a more realistic picture of your partner and yourself, (2) judge how accepting you are of each other's imperfections, and (3) learn that privacy in certain matters is acceptable.

To ensure that you will obtain this insight:

1. DO gear your secret-telling to the same disclosure level of the other person. Look for a closely aligned need to know and share the same kinds of information.

2. DO be suspicious if you don't meet your mate's friends and coworkers or visit his or her home.

3. DO expound on a secret that you have told during the idealization stage if only half the story was revealed and the rest is pertinent to your relationship.

4. DON'T blame your mate for a conflict that exists between you two if it is your fault.

5. DO observe your lover's behavior. It can be an important clue to his or her background or personality. If you think something is amiss, ask about your perceptions. You may uncover something that you should know about.

6. DO realize that you have a right to privacy if your secrets do not affect the relationship in a negative way.

7. DO evaluate the information you have gathered about your lover. Ask yourself if this person meets your needs and if you can live with the traits that irritate you.

8. DO reach a point in the realization stage where you both feel that you know the essential secrets of each other's lives.

The secrecy/disclosure patterns of the realization stage can help you and your lover see each other for the people you truly are while you maintain a sense of privacy. Should you find that you complement one another's needs and care about fulfilling them, you will consider the final stage of a romantic relationship, commitment, which entails either marriage or living together.

Commitment

As you move from the realization stage into real commitment, your use of secrecy and disclosure can become the mortar that bonds you together or the solvent that facilitates the disintegration process.

In no other stage is disclosure so consistent and intimate.

Feeling that your mate is your closest confidant can be satisfying and supportive. At times, however, it can also be problematic. The way to avoid trouble is to call upon a new group of secrecy/disclosure patterns. They include variations on some earlier categories as well as several that are unique to this phase. These patterns are Mutual Confidences, Previous Indiscretions and Private Secrets, Present Problems, Vengeful Weapons, and Playful Toys.

MUTUAL CONFIDENCES

Many couples share a secret they wouldn't like even their families or closest friends to know. Although the hidden situation may involve only one of the pair, both decide to remain silent. Their love and acceptance have sealed them in a secrecy pact.

When problems are caused by these secretive agreements, they can be solved if the partners work together toward a solution.

One afternoon I received a phone call while I was on the radio. A man, identifying himself as Jerry, said he was upset because his ex-wife, Susanna, was threatening to blackmail him. She had just seen his new wife with a lesbian lover in a gay bar and unless he paid her a thousand dollars, she would tell his parents.

Jerry was panicked. He didn't want his mother or father to know what he had known for some time. He admitted that he would have preferred Renée to be heterosexual, but he loved her so much that he was willing to share her periodically.

I helped Jerry understand that he had more control in this situation than he thought. I suggested that he refuse to be blackmailed, and if Susanna did spread the secret around, he and Renée could deny it as a filthy rumor. If he gave in to her and paid the money, Susanna would have proof that this was indeed a spicy situation worth her time and effort to pursue. He understood my point.

A few days later, when Jerry called back, he reported that he and Renée had refused to pay his ex-wife any money to keep quiet. He added that, to his amazement, she had backed down. In addition, the experience had brought him closer to Renée. She still planned to see her lover, but she told Jerry how her feelings for him had grown.

This troublesome episode worked out because Jerry and Renée were honest with each other before marriage. If she had kept her bisexuality a secret, this news from Jerry's ex-wife would have come as a terrible shock to him. He would have felt duped and perhaps even sought a divorce.

A secrecy pact can help you prevent a private matter from being uncovered. The trust that you place in each other because of this mutual secret usually increases the relationship's intimate bonding.

PREVIOUS INDISCRETIONS AND PRIVATE SECRETS

As we have seen, you should not tell all your secrets to a person before you make a commitment. Some confidences are just too threatening to disclose. Others seem like only your personal business and nobody else's. And then there are the secrets that you have been told confidentially by others.

Should your feelings about personal privacy change when you marry or live together? Only to a degree. What held true in the realization secrecy/disclosure pattern, To Tell or Not to Tell, also fits in this stage. Even though you have become truly connected with another person, you do not have to be secretless, nor should you feel guilty about withholding some information.

Still, you may want to be more straightforward about yourself than you have been in the previous stages. After all, the better your spouse or lover knows you, the more accepted and loved you can feel.

In general, where your personal life is concerned, you should be the judge. Just remember that previous indiscretions and private thoughts or experiences that are too threatening to reveal can remain yours alone if they are not causing relationship troubles.

An example of a secret that may be your business alone and therefore kept from the special person in your life is your sexual fantasies. You can use some exciting thoughts during sex to help things along . . . that's perfectly OK. The other person does not have to know.

If, however, your sexual fantasies have a bizarre nature, try to analyze what they might mean. They may indicate problems with intimacy (remember Rebecca's battling women fantasy) that you should talk over with a mental health professional.

There is one more side to this confidentiality issue. It revolves around the secrets others share with you but not with your mate. Should a friend, neighbor or offspring swear you to secrecy, it's better not to tell your partner even though you think confiding would be a harmless gesture. Remember, your life has many attachments and you have a responsibility in each one to be supportive and trustworthy. If you don't want to keep secrets from your mate, don't promise not to tell when others approach you with personal information.

The Previous Indiscretions and Private Secrets patterns can take the guesswork out of interpersonal secrecy with your partner, yourself, and those who are special in your life.

PRESENT PROBLEMS

As time passes, you change and so does your mate. Will you share those changes with each other? One would hope so, but there is pressure to conceal information to maintain the relationship's status quo or to prevent a partner from being hurt.

Secrets that arise between spouses or lovers during the course of the commitment stage are usually kept with the best intentions. Unfortunately, many of these confidences interfere with intimacy.

Problematic secrets must be faced, but they do not have to be told to your significant other. You could open up to a friend, as Dominic did, and find a solution to what is bothering you.

Dominic loved Jonelle very much. They had been married for several years. Recently, Dominic had found himself too tired or too uninterested to have sex as often as they used to in the early part of their relationship. Still, Dominic was known as a macho man and felt his image required that he always be ready for sex.

Not wanting to disappoint Jonelle or ruin his image, Dominic began faking orgasms. Initially, doing this seemed to solve the problem, but then he began to feel resentful.

One evening after work, he stopped for a few beers with his friend Jack. First Jack confided in Dominic some personal problems with his in-laws. Then, all of a sudden, Dominic found himself pouring out his secret. He took the risk of being laughed at and asked Jack for advice.

Jack asked why Dominic wasn't as turned on to Jonelle as he used to be. Dominic hadn't thought about it that way. He realized that he felt she didn't care as much for him as before because she was spending so much time on her career.

Jack suggested that Dominic not confess his secret to Jonelle but rather talk to her about his frustrations with her time-consuming work and see where that led.

A week later, when they met again for drinks, Dominic told Jack that he had shared his concerns with his wife. She had reacted in a positive way and promised to spend more time at home. She had been carried away, she said, by her boss's expectations of her in the office and had been neglecting her marriage. She also admitted that she had missed the closeness she and Dominic once shared.

Dominic felt so much better and so much less resentful that he found he didn't need to fake any sexual responses. The problem underlying his need for secrecy had been solved.

It is important to monitor new secrets that may be building between you and your mate. If they are potential trouble, it is wise to deal with them early. Otherwise, you may hide changing needs and repress the feelings that come from not having them met. The end result can be disharmony where there was once accord.

VENGEFUL WEAPONS

Living with a person can create conflict as well as intimacy. In those instances where you each compete for what you think is right, you are apt to use many different ploys to win your case.

While secrets can be called upon to prove your point or put your

mate in his or her place, it's better not to use this Vengeful se-
crecy/disclosure pattern. It only destroys your partner's confidence
in you and damages your relationship.

Marie chose this category to take vengeance against Bud, who had
been verbally and physically abusive to her for years. One afternoon, Marie's hostility surfaced when Bud slapped her and called
her stupid. She struck back, not with her fists, but with a long-
concealed love affair. She described how she had fallen passionately
for another man shortly after she married Bud.

Her husband refused to believe her at first, but he soon realized
that she was telling the truth. He was shocked and upset. Marie rel-
ished every moment of his pain. She was delighted as he retreated in
defeat and she advanced, victorious.

From that day on, the marriage changed. Bud no longer abused
her, but he did begin to mistrust her. Today their marriage is still
filled with tension. Unless they work through their feelings, the relationship is not likely to improve.

The Vengeful pattern must be avoided at all cost because both
partners lose. If you feel like using a secret against your mate, rethink your motivation. Your urge is probably being triggered by a
problem within the relationship. It would be best to deal with that
conflict head-on either together or with professional help. Otherwise, you are practically ensuring a loveless match.

PLAYFUL TOYS

Up to now, we have been looking at secrecy and disclosure in a serious context. You have seen how it can make or break an intimate attachment.

Let's turn and focus on secrecy exclusively because it can add
spice to your relationship by creating mystery.

Peggy loved to surprise her husband, James, when he returned
from his long business trips. Although they spoke on the phone
while he was away, she would never tell him what to expect when
he returned. Sometimes she would have a special present waiting.
Other times, she would change her hair and makeup or prepare a
night of sexual fun by redecorating their bedroom in a fantasy
theme.

Needless to say, James never lingered at the airport upon his arrival home. He and Peggy had discovered the spicy aspect of secrecy.

You can be playful with secrets during any stage of a romantic relationship, but you will find it easiest and most useful in this phase. Why? Because you have learned what pleasure you both like, and you need some stimulation to keep the relationship alive and well.

In the commitment stage, these five patterns — Mutual Confidences, Previous Indiscretions and Private Secrets, Present Problems, Vengeful Weapons, and Playful Toys — can be helpful in four ways. They can (1) encourage you to protect your privacy when appropriate, (2) prompt you to reveal new secrets that may become problematic, (3) help you to identify if a disclosure is being used as a weapon, and (4) allow you to enjoy playful secretive behavior.

To use these patterns effectively:

1. DON'T tell your mate everything. You deserve some privacy within the relationship so that you can remain an individual with a clear sense of self. For this reason, don't expect total honesty from your partner.

2. DON'T use disclosure as a weapon to take revenge against your spouse or lover. You will both end up losers.

3. DO let secrecy be a playful toy. It can keep your relationship fanciful, young and alive.

4. DO reveal any secret that you have kept during the idealization and realization stages that could affect your commitment in a negative way.

5. DO treasure beneficial secrecy pacts and work together to prevent their discovery by others.

6. DON'T feel guilty about keeping a friend's, neighbor's, or offspring's confidence from your mate if you have promised to do so.

7. DO be aware that new secrets may crop up between the two of you. When they do, deal with the troublesome ones quickly so they won't cause problems.

The secrecy/disclosure patterns of the commitment stage can make a dramatic difference in your relationship. When you begin relying on them, you will find that you can be a private person within an interpersonal bond. You will also discover that you can increase the intimacy that you share by revealing the deeply personal side of your life.

A NEW INTIMACY

Idealization, realization, and commitment are wonderful stages in a romantic relationship. Each deserves to be savored bringing with it new interpersonal adventures.

Secrecy/disclosure can intensify the thrill of being with another person because it helps you share yourself and remain an individual.

In the past you may have found that secrets were a problem because you were either too open or too closed with your lover or spouse. You are now ready to change all that. You know the purpose of secrecy and disclosure and how concealing and revealing personal information can protect your privacy and increase intimacy.

I would encourage you to experiment with the patterns that we have discussed. By your using them, your relationship will enter a new realm of understanding, individuality, and love.

9

Confiding in Authorities

PATRICK REILLY, M.D., was a respected and successful physician. He was also a drug addict.

Every morning as he made his rounds at the hospital, and each afternoon when he saw his patients in his private office, he put their lives, his medical center's reputation, and his career in jeopardy.

No one knew of Dr. Reilly's addiction to prescription drugs. Not his teachers, his superiors, nor his psychiatrist.

In the book *A Private Practice*, Dr. Reilly (a pseudonym) detailed how the pressures of medical school triggered his drug dependency: "Anxiety struck like a thunderbolt. And struck repeatedly. Daily. Hourly. Depression settled in, suffocating me. . . . How could I perform in medical school if I couldn't sleep?"

After graduation, Dr. Reilly's addiction intensified. For fourteen years, his daily ritual of pill taking was his defense against the pressures of his job. Eventually panic attacks, bouts of forgetfulness, and impotency began to cause him to lose control of his professional and personal life. When he misdiagnosed a case of spinal meningitis, he was sufficiently shaken to admit the truth to his psychiatrist and to himself.

Dr. Reilly enrolled in a drug rehabilitation program and began to experience the different phases of fear, anger, and denial on his road to recovery. As a doctor, he found it particularly difficult to be a patient and accept advice from other physicians. His inability to work with the substance abuse advisors compounded his efforts to rid himself of the addiction. Finally, it was the honesty and support of the other patients in the program that made the difference and he began to make progress.

In reading Dr. Reilly's book, I found it significant that he could relate to his fellow patients at the drug rehabilitation center but not to the counselors. Perhaps the situation had less to do with his position as a physician and more to do with his history of being anxious and secretive around authority figures.

The fear of not doing well and not being accepted by his superiors no doubt contributed to his need to disguise his insecurities and hide his drug dependency. He reconsidered his priorities only when a patient's life and his own were placed in severe danger. Dr. Reilly had become frightened that he could no longer function effectively. He realized his secret would soon be uncovered and, if a patient died because of it, the ramifications could be catastrophic.

AUTHORITY FIGURE PLUS ANXIETY LEVEL EQUALS SECRECY/DISCLOSURE RESPONSE

Do you ever feel anxious around an authority figure such as a policeman, lawyer, employer, professor, loan officer, or clergyman? Does that anxiety level increase when you are asked to relate to the person in a stressful situation that is personally threatening? For example, do you become tense if you must report to your boss, respond to a subpoena, or talk to a clergyman about something you have done wrong?

We all experience stress, to one degree or another, when we are with superiors. Anxiety is a natural reaction because we feel that their position makes them powerful. Since we need their support, we want to present an acceptable image. The fear of being rejected, ridiculed, or punished stimulates an anxiety level that prompts one of the two extremes of secretive or nonsecretive behavior. Our response is to protect ourselves either by being too open or too closed with personal information.

If you tend to have an inappropriately open nature you usually reveal secrets to an authority figure because you perceive the individual as someone on your side and as a person who will shield you from criticism if he or she knows all the facts.

Should you tend to have a too closed nature, you conceal information from an authority because you consider the person to be negative or hostile toward you, and you feel you can protect yourself from the individual's disapproval by telling him or her very little.

It appears that Dr. Reilly was too closed. His secretiveness trapped him in destructive behavior.

To understand how being too open can be problematic, we need only to consider Carvill, a woman who was always very verbal when confronted by her superiors, a law enforcement officer, or a professional. She frequently exposed information that could have been left unsaid.

One day, Carvill was stopped by a highway patrolman. She had been speeding and she knew it. As he approached the car, her palms began to sweat. Carvill rolled down her window with dread and looked up at the uniformed figure staring down at her. In the next instant she blurted out, "I'm sorry, officer. I didn't mean to run those three stop signs too." As he removed his sunglasses he answered, "I only pulled you over for driving eighty in a fifty-five-mile-per-hour zone. I didn't see the other offenses."

Carvill was given four citations. By confessing impulsively to everything she had done, she created more trouble for herself.

Do you identify with Dr. Reilly's or Carvill's reaction to authority? You are probably not as extreme as either and fall on the Secrecy/Disclosure Scale somewhere between their highly closed and highly open natures. Still, you may feel that what you have concealed or revealed to superiors or professionals in the past has created problems in your life.

You can prevent further trouble by learning how to handle secrets when you are with authorities. By developing your secrecy/disclosure skills in this area, you can take another step toward modifying your too open or too closed nature so that it is more balanced.

To make the appropriate secrecy/disclosure choices, you must know the reasons for keeping and telling secrets around an authority figure, the ways to reduce your anxiety level during an encounter, and the secrecy/disclosure pattern that is most likely at play during a confrontation.

REASONS FOR SECRECY/DISCLOSURE

There are occasions when it is important to keep secrets from your employer, consultants, and law enforcement officials, but there are other times when it is essential to speak up.

You can end the confusion of the secrecy/disclosure choice by asking yourself: Is my motivation to conceal or reveal this information appropriate?

To answer that question you need to know the reasons for keeping or telling secrets when you are with an authority.

When to Conceal

Secrets that are withheld from your boss, a consultant, or law enforcement officials can be powerful tools for advancement on the job, prestige in the community, or protection of your image. You are wise to guard your privacy when it benefits you and others in a nondestructive way.

In general, concealment is appropriate when it helps you:

- get ahead by protecting an aspect of your ability that could be interpreted as problematic,
- avoid unjust punishment by shielding you from an apparent involvement in socially unacceptable behavior,
- protect others who have requested your confidentiality,
- stop unnecessary scrutiny of a harmless idiosyncrasy that could be misinterpreted as a drawback to your acceptance.

You will want to keep a secret from an authority figure if you sense the information will cause you to be misjudged. You need not feel guilty about your concealment decision if it does not put people in danger, stunt your personal or professional growth, or harm your emotional well-being.

When to Reveal

Information you tell an authority can strengthen your abilities, broaden your resources, prevent you from being hurt, and establish you as a trusted individual.

Disclosure is advantageous when you receive one or more of the following from an authority figure:

- guidance and assistance to better your skills, physical condition, emotional well-being, or general livelihood;
- protection against individuals or forces that could harm you;
- loyalty and support to help you pursue a goal;
- acceptance and respect that enable you to be viewed as a valuable person.

It is best to reveal a confidence if the information will create stronger bonds with authorities or help them in matters that will improve your life.

The next time you are with your employer or advisors, or have an encounter with a law enforcement official you will want to remember these reasons for secrecy or disclosure. By weighing the pros and cons of being open or closed you can make the appropriate concealment or revelation choice.

RELATIONSHIPS WITH AUTHORITIES

What type of relationship do you have with authority figures? Do you relate with ease or with discomfort? Do you tend to follow their lead or consider only your own needs?

The second step in managing secrets and disclosures with authorities is to feel secure in their presence. Although they may have more expertise than you, you share something in common. You are adults. If you deal with them on an equal level of maturity, you will not feel threatened, your anxiety level will be low, and you will act less impulsively.

Most of us experience problems when we are with authority figures because we become childlike in their presence. We give them too much control. In many instances, this upper hand turns them into a parental power. We allow ourselves to become overly dependent or terribly frightened, and our basic childhood secretive or nonsecretive nature of being too closed or too open becomes magnified. It is then that we say too little or too much.

There are three factors that influence this response to authority: your past relationship with your parents, the authority's individual personality, and your present state of mind.

Parental Influence

The anxiety level you feel when you are around superiors and professionals depends a great deal on your experiences with those very first authorities, your father and mother. In chapters 4, 5, 6 and 7, you considered the type of home environment in which you were raised. You saw how the rigidity or flexibility of that atmosphere had an effect on your secrecy/disclosure nature. Now let's look at how it influenced your future dealings with employers and professionals.

As an adult you tend to perceive authority figures in a fashion similar to the way you saw your parents, though in reality, they may be very different from your mother and father.

In effect, when you face an authority you become a child again and your juvenile anxiety blurs your judgment. You interact in the way that won parental approval or at least achieved self-protection.

Think about how strict, lenient, or inconsistent your parents were in disciplining you as you were growing up. Ask yourself how that treatment has influenced your present feelings about authority.

If your mother and father were very strict disciplinarians you may find that your most recent experience with a superior or a professional left you being too secretive for your own good. Should your parents have been more like friends to you and really never set limits or dealt out punishment, your last meeting with an authority may have had you telling everything without consideration for adequate protection against the individual's power or influence.

The third possibility is that either you were raised by a series of people with different degrees of rigidity or you had parents who gave you conflicting messages about discipline. Sometimes they may have been very strict and at other times they may have been too permissive. As an adult you may vacillate in your reactions to and feelings about authority figures.

You can modify your childlike reactions and reduce your anxiety level when you are with an authority in the following ways:

1. Think consciously about what your relationship was like with your parents.
2. Make an effort not to duplicate this behavior with the present authority figure.
3. Think before you reveal or conceal information, noting your adult needs and what you think this person's response will be to your revelation.

These three guidelines can help you deal with any regression to childlike behavior that an employer or professional might stimulate.

The Individual Personality of the Authority Figure

In reality, of course, not all authority figures are alike. Some, more than others, are apt to make you throw rationality to the wind and react as though you were a child again. A few push your buttons because they bear a physical resemblance to your parents, others because their manner or way of relating brings back distant memories of teachers, scoutmasters, or other childhood authority figures.

If you are aware of these factors and analyze them, they will help you get your anxiety level under control.

Present State of Mind

In addition to your upbringing and the personality of the authority figure, your emotional well-being can affect how you relate to superiors and professionals. It is wise to consider how vulnerable you are when you are talking to an authority. If you don't, you may tell the individual too much and lose control of the situation. Or, you could withhold information that puts you at a disadvantage.

A divorce, financial loss, or a loved one's death can leave you emotionally vulnerable. The lawyer, loan officer, or undertaker is supposed to offer comfort and advice, but, depending on your secretive or nonsecretive nature you may not be able to judge if you are being well served.

Should you be on the open end of the Secrecy/Disclosure Scale and find yourself vulnerable when consulting an authority, you could begin to think of the individual as a savior or fantasy parent. Once you put the person on a pedestal, it will be difficult for you to protect your privacy. You will become more impulsively open than usual and you will leave too much to the advisor's discretion. That could lead you to assume, for example, that whatever the services cost is appropriate.

If you are on the closed end of the Secrecy/Disclosure Scale and find yourself upset emotionally, you could withdraw from the authority figure that you have consulted. Feeling insecure and worried about possible criticism, you may withhold information that could help you solve your problem. As a result the advisor could misread your reaction as hostility and refuse to help you or, in some cases, take revenge and hurt you.

Consider your level of vulnerability the next time you are working with an employer or professional. It plays an important role in how receptive you are and how effective your relationship will be.

To gauge your state of mind, you might ask yourself the following questions:

1. How do I feel emotionally when I am with this authority?
2. How dependent on this person do I want to be?
3. Am I saying too much or not enough to achieve my goal?
4. Am I asking too many or too few questions?
5. Should I get a second opinion?
6. Would having a friend at these meetings be helpful?
7. Am I relating like an adult to this authority or like a defenseless or offensive child?
8. Am I attaining my goal?

Being able to identify if you are in a vulnerable state of mind will help you work better with an authority. You can monitor your reactions or ask a friend to assist you in handling your problem.

You now know the reasons for keeping silent or speaking up when you are with your boss, a law enforcement official, or an advisor. You have seen how parental influence, the individual authority's personality, and your state of mind can affect your relationships with superiors and professionals.

When you begin to use this knowledge you will lower your anxiety level and modify your response whenever you are confronted by an authority.

THE DILEMMA OF CHOICE

The final step in learning to handle secrets and disclosures with authorities is to understand the secrecy/disclosure patterns that are most often at work. There are basically four types of revelation and concealment choices that recur under certain circumstances and during specific encounters.

I have named those patterns Getting Ahead, Helpful or Not, Self-Protection, and Loyalty. Each one requires that you make a decision, and that action can cause a dilemma if you are unsure about whether it is better to conceal or reveal the information.

To take the guesswork out of keeping and telling secrets in these situations, I would like you to consider four case histories, four dilemmas, and four solutions. They will show you how the secrecy/disclosure patterns work and will give you the guidelines for dealing with them in the future.

Getting Ahead

The job market is highly competitive. If you are to remain upwardly mobile, you sometimes find it necessary to maintain a front or image. You realize it is important to appear efficient and strong because those are the traits an employer usually values in an employee.

DILEMMA: What if a personal or professional problem threatens to undermine your productivity? Do you tell your boss or keep quiet?

CASE HISTORY 1

Randy had a good job with an international conglomerate. She had been steadily promoted ever since joining the company seven years ago. Her boss liked her style and had recently told her she was in line for another promotion.

One night after returning from a business trip, Randy felt a lump in her breast. She was frightened and told her husband. He arranged for a medical examination. Within weeks, Randy was in the hospital having a radical mastectomy for breast cancer. Her boss, aware of the surgery, agreed to give Randy an extended leave. He also said that when she returned, he would put through the promotion.

Randy went back to work expecting everything to be as it had been before the operation. She felt her honesty with her employer had paid off. She then discovered she was mistaken. Her promotion had been given to someone else. She was told that her illness might make it difficult for her to perform at her previous level. Randy argued that her prognosis was excellent, but her boss refused to change his mind.

Recently Randy was assigned a new job with the company, but it has sidelined her for future growth. This lateral move has left her thinking about leaving the corporation. It has also made her vow to be more discriminating whenever she confides in her boss.

What happened to Randy is not unusual. Many employers have trouble dealing with an employee's recovery process after a physical or mental health problem. Even though the future may seem bright, the boss is afraid to take a risk.

If you are in a dilemma about what to tell your superior about a situation that could affect your productivity or physical stamina:

- Do think twice about the ramifications of being open with your employer.
- Do reveal the information only if you must in order either to explain reduced productivity or to ask for some special consideration related to your condition.

Your boss has no obligation to treat you like a benevolent parent or supportive mate. He or she is out to ensure profits through greater productivity. Don't make the mistake of thinking that work is a home away from home.

Helpful or Not

We seek professional advice when we are uncomfortable about something in our personal life. Initially, we want to be honest about ourselves so we can discover what is causing the distress. Frequently all seems to go well until we are actually sitting in front of the advisor, be it a clergyman, lawyer, or therapist. Then we may be intimidated by the consultant's behavior or reaction. As a result our secrecy/disclosure decisions can be adversely affected.

DILEMMA: How do you identify and handle what might be considered abusive behavior from an authority who is supposed to be advising you?

CASE HISTORY 2

Tess started seeing a therapist on the sly. She didn't want her husband or her friends to know. She was sure they would think she was crazy and would wonder why she didn't confide in them. Tess also neglected to tell her therapist that she was keeping the visits a secret for fear of criticism.

Shortly after she began therapy, the psychologist fell asleep during her session. A few weeks later he did it again and, in addition, he gave her much less time than her allotted fifty minutes.

Tess said nothing to him about his unethical behavior. She reasoned that it was her fault. He must be punishing her, she felt, because she was either too secretive or too boring. Tess began to compound matters by refusing to answer any personal questions when he was awake and counseling her.

Eventually Tess left the therapist because he was paying little attention to her, and she wasn't discussing the problem that made her go into therapy. A few months later, Tess began consulting me, and we explored her strong fear of personal judgment. She began to see how trying to avoid criticism, even from a mental health professional, had kept her closed to personal growth.

Whenever you consult an authority you will need to watch the person's behavior and response to you. To ensure that you don't make Tess's mistake:

- Do review the consultant's credentials and, if possible, talk with previous clients.
- Do meet with the advisor before you agree on a long-term professional relationship. Use this initial encounter to see how you feel about the person. Ask what will be expected of you.
- Do continue to monitor the relationship. If anything begins to happen that makes you uneasy, bring it up for discussion. The advisor may have stepped beyond the bounds of professionalism, or, on the other hand, the feelings may merely indicate that you are getting to the root of a difficult problem. If your uneasiness persists, seek a second opinion.
- Don't allow yourself to be abused. Report the behavior to the proper regulatory association or agency and seek the service elsewhere.

Responsible professionals are interested in your problems and in helping you solve them. Periodically, you may find a person who is not as professional as he or she should be. If you feel you are being abused, you are wise to take action, because if you don't, neither of you will benefit from the association.

Self-Protection

It can be unnerving when you are asked by an authority to discuss another person's private life and your involvement with the individual. Your first reaction may be to shield both of you, but after some thought you become confused. You realize that your revelation could be helpful. It may, for example, assist lawyers or the police in preventing you from being harmed. Or it may enable you to gain what is rightfully yours.

DILEMMA: How much of another person's background should you discuss with an authority?

CASE HISTORY 3

Alexis was divorcing her husband on grounds of infidelity. She hired an attorney who had been highly recommended and whom she had seen socially at the country club. Alexis had no idea that the lawyer disliked her soon-to-be ex-husband and had always been attracted to her.

The attorney began asking Alexis questions about her marriage. He said he needed to build a strong case. In her vulnerable state, she didn't realize how personal the questions were getting. She was soon discussing her husband's business dealings. Then one day, the attorney called and suggested that he and Alexis have dinner. He said there were a few points he needed to go over with her.

Alexis didn't think twice about his request for an evening meeting. She knew he was busy and she appreciated the additional attention. That night Alexis's eyes were opened finally when he suggested a nightcap at his place. She realized he was taking advantage of her vulnerability. Upset about all the personal information she had told him, she became concerned that he might use it against her.

A few days later, Alexis hired another attorney. Their relationship was strictly businesslike and he asked only pertinent questions. He also contacted Alexis's former lawyer and stressed that if any of the information Alexis had told him in confidence became common knowledge, he would be sued and taken before the American Bar Association.

You need to be cautious when you are asked to talk about someone else's private life. You may be angry at the person or frightened, but a past relationship does carry responsibility.

In general, when you are faced with discussing another person with an authority:

- Do verify the professional's credentials. Meet with previous clients or those who have had consultations with the

person. Inquire whether any private information was misused.
- Do check if the authority has a connection in the past with you or the person you will be discussing. Consider whether there may be a conflict of interest or a vendetta.
- Do set a goal for yourself. Outline the case that you must present to achieve your objective. Question what facts need to be known and which will be made public.
- Don't disclose anything that is irrelevant.
- Do make certain you know your rights. If they are infringed upon, take the proper legal steps.

Using these guidelines, you should be able to help a professional and yourself without invading anyone's privacy in a destructive manner.

Loyalty

Sharing a confidence with your boss may make you feel important and trusted. A secrecy pact between you may signal a turning point in your career. It could create stronger professional ties and position you as a valuable person within an organization.

Secrecy pacts with employers are also risky, and you must be careful before you become involved in one. They can be as destructive as they are constructive. It all depends on your relationship with your boss, the content of the secret, and what you or your superior could do with the privileged information.

DILEMMA: When should you enter into a secrecy pact with your boss?

CASE HISTORY 4

Laura was a compulsive shopper. In one year she piled up so many debts that she began embezzling from her employer's company. When she was caught finally, Laura begged her boss to forgive her. She explained that she was getting professional help and had been motivated to change.

After listening to Laura's story, her boss agreed to keep her on staff. She had been a valuable employee and since she had agreed to pay back the $15,000, he would let the incident pass. It would be their secret.

Several years later, Laura had risen within the company to become her employer's administrative assistant. In that time she had also repaid the money. She still enjoyed her work, but her life had changed. Laura had fallen in love and was planning to relocate to the West Coast with her husband-to-be.

Complications set in when she tried to leave her job. Her boss refused to accept her resignation. He admitted that he had always loved her and couldn't bear to let her leave him or the company. If she did, he threatened he would tell everyone about the embezzlement episode.

Thinking she needed psychological help, Laura contacted me for counseling. I recommended she speak with a lawyer. I pointed out that she had curbed her spending habit and paid for her mistake. There was no reason why the secrecy pact with her boss should lead to blackmail.

Laura did contact an attorney and freed herself from her employer's trap. She then moved to California with her new husband, found a job, and decided to be careful about making secrecy pacts with her new boss.

If it appears that you are about to share a mutual confidence with your superior:

- Do consider the content of the secret carefully. Judge whether or not it involves you in some dangerous kind of situation.
- Do think about the consequences if the information becomes known.
- Do be aware of any pressures you may be put under to keep the confidence.
- Do evaluate how loyalty to your boss could influence your future with the company, especially if he or she leaves because of the secret's content.
- Don't agree to a secrecy pact if you feel uncomfortable. Break off the conversation the moment you sense that collusion will put you in danger or give your employer too much power over you.

You do need your boss's support to move ahead in your job, but make sure the support you give and receive involves you in safe secrets. Then, if they become known, neither you nor the company will be harmed.

When you use these four patterns — Getting Ahead, Helpful or Not, Self-Protection, and Loyalty — in the appropriate manner, you can take the confusion out of concealing and revealing information around authorities. The next time you meet with your superior or a professional, you will want to consider which pattern is at play. Once you have identified the one that will be affecting you, recall the dos and don'ts of that category. They can help you make a revelation or concealment choice without a dilemma.

THE ENCOUNTER

You now have the secrecy/disclosure skills to deal with authorities. You know the reasons for keeping and telling secrets, how to reduce your anxiety level, and how to make the appropriate secrecy/disclosure decision.

Although your initial meetings with your boss and other professionals may be a bit rocky when you are using these techniques, keep trying. With a little practice you will find all that changing, and in the process your too open or too closed nature will become more balanced in this area. Soon you will feel free to be an individual around authorities and react to them like an adult.

Not long ago I was riding the subway and sat next to a man who had found a good balance between what to tell and what not to tell his superiors.

As the New York City subway train was about to leave the station, the conductor announced over the loudspeaker, "Watch the closing doors. Have a nice day and smile at the person sitting next to you."

The gentlemen on my right and I exchanged shy smiles and then he said, "You know I work for the Transit Authority and I should report that conductor. He's not allowed to say things like that." After a moment of introspection, he continued, "Sure, I feel better.

He even got me to smile, but my boss would want me to write him up. I don't know what to do. It's eating me up inside."

At the next stop, he stood up and said to no one in particular, "I'm not going to say a thing. What he does doesn't hurt anybody. As far as I'm concerned, it's between me and the conductor." Then I heard him add, almost under his breath, "I'm going to do something about that rule."

IO

The Last Chance to Keep and Tell

"I killed your father."

Elsie's words broke through the room's stillness and startled Lee. He looked over at his mother, who was dying of cancer. It was the first time she had spoken since he arrived that morning.

Lee moved nearer to her bed. He was shocked by her physical condition and upset that she had kept the illness a secret. He asked the Sister of Charity if the medication was making his mother delirious.

The nun shook her head and said, "Your mother has been restless for days. It started when she learned she had only a week left. It was then she asked for you. She told me there was something she had to say."

After the sister left the room, Elsie gripped Lee's sleeve and whispered, "I thought my cooking would make your father healthy again. He was so sick and thin after his heart attack."

Lee listened as his mother continued her confession. She told how she had prepared meals for his father, Art. She explained that most were left uneaten. One day she cooked a big breakfast, set an elaborate table, and demanded that Art get up and enjoy it. When he refused, she pulled him out of bed. While she was dragging him through the living room he dropped dead.

"I didn't mean to kill him," Elsie wept. "Please forgive me."

Lee assured his mother that there was nothing to forgive. He reminded her that Art was almost gone when the hospital released him. "You were just trying to keep him alive the best way you knew."

Then Lee felt the urge to tell his mother *his* secret. He admitted that he had had trouble dealing with his father's illness. For that reason he hadn't been able to visit him during those final months. Lee apologized.

Elsie smiled sympathetically. She said that there was nothing he could have done.

As Lee held his mother's hand, she seemed to relax. Their conversation had put things in perspective for her. Soon Elsie settled into a deep sleep, from which she never awakened.

MAKING PEACE

Elsie had some unfinished business to take care of before she died. She needed to talk about her role in the unusual circumstances surrounding her husband's death. She wanted to clear her conscience and be forgiven for her actions and her angry feelings toward her dying spouse.

Since Art's massive coronary eight years ago, she had estranged herself from Lee. The decision to break away grew out of a fear that he would discover her "crime." The schism had become so deep that she had chosen to die alone in a hospice, a community designed to meet the special needs of the terminally ill.

By telling her secret, Elsie finally accepted the reality that she did not kill her husband. She became reunited with her son and died in peace. Lee also benefited. Elsie's deathbed disclosure prompted him to discuss his own guilt feelings surrounding his father's heart attack. Although their confessions had been traumatic, they had both put the past to rest.

THE LAST CHANCE

In many instances, people feel that the deathbed is their last opportunity to reveal a secret. No matter how open or closed their nature, they will be more open than usual during the dying process. Their need to be truly known encourages them to disclose confidences before either they die or a loved one dies.

Sharing secrets at this stressful time can be an enriching experience as it was for Elsie and Lee. They were able to realize the benefits of deathbed disclosure:

- clearing a conscience,
- reconciling with a loved one,
- releasing anxiety and guilt,
- enabling one to be known and accepted.

They avoided the distress and trauma that deathbed revelations can cause, because Elsie had considered what she wanted to say, had timed her confession so she still was able to discuss it, and had concluded that her admission would not hurt Lee after she had passed away.

SECRET-SPILLING

Deathbed secrets can create problems if the dying person or those who are experiencing the loss begin telling confidences impulsively. This secret-spilling is triggered by the sickroom's stillness and its accompanying emotional tension. Personal awkwardness and anxiety push people into filling the silence with all types of confessions. Experiences that should be left in the past become common knowledge and have the potential of causing severe repercussions. Later, people may regret what they have said, but the damage has already been done.

When secrets are told indiscriminately around the deathbed they can be very destructive because they:

- hurt feelings,
- harm personal images,
- create interpersonal rifts.

These side effects can leave those involved emotionally devastated. Instead of being at peace with each other, they feel as if they are at war.

There is no reason why deathbed secrecy/disclosure behavior

needs to be a terribly traumatic experience. It could be, though, if you tend to have either a too open or too closed nature. You may find that you will be more impulsive than usual or that you will make mistakes because you are not used to revealing confidences.

To ensure that sharing secrets around the deathbed is a positive experience, you must be prepared. The best way is to write a will and, in the process, modify your too open or too closed nature so that it is more balanced for this occasion. By using the document when needed, you will reveal confidences appropriately and to the proper beneficiaries.

A PERSONAL SECRETS WILL

If you had ten days to live, what confidences would you share?

If you knew someone who was dying, what would you want to discuss?

Would your revealed secrets create stronger bonds or deeper schisms?

Don't worry if you find these questions disconcerting or hard to answer. You are not alone. The general subject of death and dying is anxiety-provoking. Few of us want to think of our own mortality or the loss of a loved one. Unfortunately we must. Nobody lives forever. We may do everything we can to protect our health, but eventually systems break down or we meet with an accidental end.

We have heard nightmarish stories about people who have not prepared for their own death. The lack of direction about what should be done if they are physically incapacitated produces misery. The nonexistence of a will or living trust brings about confusion.

Similar despair prevails if a person is not ready for deathbed secrecy/disclosure behavior. When confidences are revealed indiscriminately, people can be needlessly hurt.

You can take the impulsiveness out of revealing secrets around the deathbed by writing a personal secrets will that has two sections. The first part will focus on you and the second on your loved ones. Preparing this confidential bequest can help you decide:

- what you want to disclose before you die,
- whom you will tell your most guarded confidences,
- how you will reveal your secrets.

The decision to deal with your hidden past now by writing your personal secrets will will take the pressure off you during the dying process. Time is on your side at this point. You can carefully evaluate what you wish to disclose and how that information will affect you and others. Having weighed the pros and cons of each confidence, you can either list it in your will or leave it out. Then, when you are on your deathbed or around a loved one's, you will know what to reveal and conceal.

In order to write your personal secrets will it is important for you to consider the types of confidences that are usually disclosed by both a dying person and an individual experiencing the loss. By being aware of these two different categories, you will be able to uncover the secrets that you want to discuss. Then when the time comes you can reread your notes and be ready to make the best of this final opportunity for disclosure.

Section I. A Dying Person's Secrets

On your deathbed, you will probably be motivated to tell long-concealed secrets because you hope to clear your conscience, be accepted for past wrongs, have the final word, or leave the world a better place. For those reasons your disclosures will tend to revolve around four specific secret categories: Past Misadventures, Reconciliation, Family History, Hurtful Moments, and Misunderstandings. Let's consider which of them you will want to put in the first section of your will.

PAST MISADVENTURES

Do you still have misgivings about something you did in the past? Are you hiding the experience from those you love because you are afraid of their reaction?

On the deathbed you will discover that the fear of rejection will no longer be as important. Your need to protect your image decreases as your desire to clear your conscience increases.

Elsie kept her secret for eight years, but when she realized that she had a week to live she decided there was no reason to be secretive anymore. She wanted to be forgiven and, although it was uncomfortable and risky to speak up, she was rewarded with peace of mind.

In preparing your personal secrets will, you need to consider any past misadventures that you have hidden. Pay particular attention to those that have distanced you from your family, mate, or close friends. Ask yourself what would happen if you disclosed the incident. Would it hurt someone who was involved and who will live on after your death? Could it relieve guilt feelings? Might it settle a rift between you and someone special?

If you have secrets that could resolve past misunderstandings or end separations without creating new problems, you will want to include them in your will.

RECONCILIATION

Is there a situation in your life fraught with friction? Has this interpersonal tension been going on for some time? Is the cause of this aggravation a well-guarded secret?

For example, an argument that is never settled can cause trouble whenever those involved get together. The repressed anger bubbles over or lies just beneath the surface.

On the deathbed, we tend to gain perspective on life. Our ego takes a back seat to our desire to leave the world a better place.

This hope to make peace was on Randall's mind as he lay dying. From his deathbed he looked over at his wife, daughter, and mother and remembered the arguments they had had over raising Timmy, his grandson. He recalled a Fourth of July disagreement six years before, when their differences had really gotten out of hand. Timmy had fallen from a tree and, after they found him unhurt, they argued about how he should be disciplined. The argument escalated into a food fight. If the women had not been pulled apart, they would have started hitting each other. Since then they had not spoken to each other except in polite interchanges at formal gatherings.

Randall brought up the incident. He could sense the tension in the room. As he began to talk about how Timmy had become a fine boy in spite of their disagreements, he began to smile. Then he asked them to make peace and forget about their "secret war." He wanted them to do it for him.

The three women looked at each other and at Randall. Minutes later they were crying in one another's arms.

Are there any unsettled arguments in your life that continue to fester? Take time to think about past quarrels. If talking over the incidents would help you be more at peace, be sure to include them in your will. List next to each argument, if there are more than one, the person or people who were involved.

FAMILY HISTORY

Do you have privileged information about your family? Is there a part of your heritage that will be forgotten or purposefully lost if you don't pass it along before you die?

Sometimes we don't wish to associate with certain members of our family. Other times we may even find our background to be a stumbling block. As we go through life, we may attempt to be independent from our family, but on the deathbed, we tend to reestablish our roots.

For example, Sam, an only child, had changed his family name when he became an adult. He felt that since it sounded Jewish, it was detrimental to his career plans. He wanted to be a banker.

Sam covered his tracks by moving away from his hometown and dissociating himself from his parents. He married and then raised his children to believe that their ancestors were English. He bought a portrait at an antique shop and claimed that it was a painting of his paternal grandfather. He even had a coat of arms designed to complement his new name.

On the deathbed, Sam experienced strong guilt feelings. He began to hate himself for lying to his wife and children and for disowning his heritage. While he was dying he told his immediate family everything about their real paternal grandparents and great-grandparents. Sam's son and daughter were shocked. They were also intrigued with the intelligence and perseverance of their ancestors. Sam explained to his children that they could do whatever they wanted with this new information. He begged them, though, never to let their real background be lost.

Your family secret may not be as dramatic as Sam's. Still, you could have information that would add perspective to your heritage for other family members. Or you may be the only person who knows certain things about the family's illnesses or causes of death. Be sure to include in your will any hidden facts about your roots, especially if you have trouble talking about them now.

HURTFUL MOMENTS

Is there a person in your life who has made you unhappy? Have you wanted to take revenge but never had the nerve?

Sometimes the deathbed becomes a war zone from which people can retaliate against those who have hurt them. They feel their vengeful behavior will be excused because they are ill. They expect to avoid all repercussions because they will soon die.

Revenge, however, is like a boomerang. It comes back to harm the person who takes the retaliatory action. This is true whether the avenging individual is healthy or not.

It is unwise to put in your will a secret that could punish someone for mistreating you. Faye's case history may help you understand why.

Faye had been raised in the shadow of her younger brother. She grew up hating her mother for giving him all the attention. Years later when Faye's illness was diagnosed as cancer, she decided to keep her illness a secret. Since she had "mothered" herself as a child, she was determined to do it again as an adult. She also planned to use her self-reliant actions to get even with her mother. She would write her a letter and explain why she had chosen to die alone. When the note was opened after her death, Faye felt her mother would be left with terrible feelings of guilt.

Half a year passed, and Faye recovered. The battle with the disease had left her a different person. She was less petty and more forgiving. Upon leaving the hospital, Faye contacted her mother and apologized for her secretive behavior.

Faye's mother was delighted to hear of her daughter's recovery and was pleased to have the chance to explain why Faye's brother had received all the attention. The prognosis at his birth gave him four years to live. She had not wanted to worry Faye about his impending death so she never mentioned it. Then it was discovered that his condition had been misdiagnosed. The revelation increased her devotion to him.

The two women reconciled. Faye was glad that she had had a second chance to settle the past. She was also thankful that she had not tried to get even. She would have left her mother with unnecessary feelings of remorse.

If you are harboring vengeful thoughts, it would be best to deal with them now. Don't wait until you are on the deathbed. You could find, as Faye did, that you have misinterpreted the situation. Disclosure could clarify the incident and give you years of anxiety-free moments with someone you love.

MISUNDERSTANDINGS

Do you project a false image of yourself? Are you uncomfortable with that facade? Do you maintain the persona because you feel you have no alternative?

Each of us presents him- or herself to the world in a special manner. In some instances not even our mate, family, or close friends know who we really are. We have decided to hide bits and pieces of our personality because we fear rejection or ridicule.

On the deathbed, people tend to drop pretensions. If you have ever wanted to reveal your true self, you may find it easier when you are dying. Burt certainly did. He had always been perceived as a noncompassionate man. Although his family asked him constantly to lighten up, he always refused.

While he was dying, Burt apologized for having been so difficult. He told his wife and children that he loved them very much but was afraid to show it. He couldn't be demonstrative because that wasn't the way he was raised. Burt felt real men never cried or showed feelings.

As his family began to hug him, Burt broke down. All the emotions that had been locked inside were released. In his final weeks, he was a different person and he and his loved ones experienced an extraordinary period of closeness.

I would encourage you to think twice before you add an image secret to your will. If the hidden information is too difficult for you to discuss now, then later might be better. But there is no reason to wait until you are dying. Ask yourself what you would lose by revealing your true self to those you love at this moment. Would it mean a stronger bond? Could the admission make you feel less defensive and more relaxed? If you answer yes to those questions, it would be a mistake to procrastinate. If your response is no, then include the secret in your will.

Devise and Bequeath

As you have been preparing Section I of your will, you probably have uncovered two different kinds of confidences: the ones you wish to reveal now and those that you will tell when you are dying.

One of the advantages of doing this exercise is discovering secrets that if disclosed now could improve your relationships. You may have found several that you want to reveal. That's terrific. The deathbed should be used only as a last resort.

If you have gathered some secrets that you will tell at the end of your life, you will want to decide two things: who are the beneficiaries and how will they be told.

Since the main purpose of deathbed secrecy/disclosure behavior is to bring you closer to loved ones, the recipients of your revelations should be the people who have been affected by your secrets. Take time to write the appropriate names alongside the confidences you plan to reveal. This will enable you to go about your disclosure in a more deliberate manner.

There are two ways you can tell your secret. You can do it either face-to-face or in a letter that is opened before or after your death. Choose whichever technique suits your purposes. A letter may be less threatening than a personal encounter in certain cases. You judge which method will work for which disclosure. Then make the proper notations next to the secrets you have listed.

You have just completed the first section of your will. You are probably looking at a series of secrets. By each one is the beneficiary or beneficiaries and the technique you plan to use when you disclose the information.

Now it is time to write the second section of your will, the one that deals with what you wish to tell loved ones who are near death.

Section II. Secrets for the Dying

As a person who is watching another die, you go through many emotions, including anger, fear, and grief. Most of those reactions occur because you feel you have no control over what is happening. All you think you can do is sit by helplessly and watch death approach.

You can be more in control at this time if you participate in the process by intensifying your relationship with the person who is about to die. Knowing in advance what you want to disclose can make a difficult experience less traumatic. You will be able to say things that could heal past differences and deepen the intimacy.

Your conversation may encourage the dying person to reveal certain secrets to you. The end result can be a deeply moving experience. You may share even more love during this period than ever before.

You can decide which secrets to tell around the deathbed by reviewing the types of disclosure that are most often told to the dying. I classify these particular secrets as Past Hurts, Hidden Changes, Life during Dying, and the Illness.

As we go through the various categories, you may be reminded of personal secrets that you want to include in your will.

PAST HURTS

What experiences have you hidden from someone who is very close to you? Has the secret caused you anguish? Have you not revealed the incident because it could upset your relationship?

When a person you love lies dying you tend to feel guilty about what you have kept hidden. Instead of carrying that guilt to your own grave, you may consider opening up.

For example, Belle's husband, Dudley, was a traveling salesman. She had hated the time he had spent on the road but had never said a word. Belle wanted him to think that she was strong enough to handle the house and the children. It was her way of letting him do his thing.

While Dudley was dying, Belle told him how lonely she had been when he was away on business trips. Dudley's reaction surprised her. He began to cry. Then he admitted that he traveled only because he thought she liked being on her own. He wished that she had told him her secret sooner. If she had, he would have asked for a different job.

Belle held Dudley's hand. Both of them felt terrible at first. Then he eased their discomfort by suggesting that at least they had finally been open with one another.

If you have a secret that is creating anxiety with someone you love and you cannot discuss it now, put it in your will. It may be less threatening to talk about near the end. The insight that you both gain could make your final days richer.

On the other hand, if Dudley's and Belle's story touches a chord in your life, think about the consequences of dealing with your secret at the moment. Perhaps it would be better to reveal the confidence as soon as possible so that you can reap the benefits of your disclosure for years and not just for a few weeks or days.

HIDDEN CHANGES

Are you the person who the dying person thinks you are? Should you ever admit that you are really different?

As you watch someone die, you often wonder if you should tell all. You may have been open in some ways but closed in others.

Although most people do become more understanding on their deathbeds, many do not. Consequently, you take a risk when you decide to reveal a guarded aspect of your personality to a dying person. Instead of being accepted, you may be rejected.

For example, Monty decided not to tell his mother about an impending divorce. She was dying and she seemed to take solace every time he and his wife visited her bedside. Monty's mother had always been proud of him. She felt a part of his success, which included an important job, a lovely wife, and four children, all of whom had gone on to college.

What Monty didn't tell his mother was that he and his wife had decided to split after twenty-three years of marriage. It was a mutual decision but one that had been delayed, first by Monty's father's death, and now by his mother's terminal illness. Monty didn't want to hurt his mother or make her worry about the family's future.

After his mother died, Monty divorced. He felt that keeping the breakup from her had been positive. It made her last days with him devoid of conflict and full of love.

You may want to exclude from your will a secret that could be unsettling to the dying person. You do have a responsibility to help your loved one die in comfort. Looking after the person's emotional well-being is part of that obligation.

If there is a hidden change in your life that you would like to reveal, and it poses little threat to the person on the deathbed, then include that secret in your will.

LIFE DURING DYING

Should you tell someone who is near death that you are enjoying life? Should you discuss vacation plans? Is it wise to keep bad news a secret?

Too often the terminally ill are protected from the ongoing ups and downs of their family and friends. This happens because those who will live on begin to feel guilty about their good fortune in the face of death. They also think they have no right to burden the dying person with their rough moments.

Your life goes on while a person is dying. Keeping that in mind is very important. Cecily found this to be true when her father was diagnosed to have an advanced heart condition. It was decided that he should be hospitalized for long-term care. After about a month, his condition stabilized and the family was told he had at least six months to live.

About at that time, Cecily's husband found he had to travel to Hawaii on business. He suggested that she and the children accompany him so that he could extend the trip into a week's vacation. Cecily wanted to go but felt guilty about enjoying herself while her father was ill.

Cecily called one afternoon while I was doing the radio show and asked what decision she should make. I uged her to go to Hawaii and to tell her father about the trip. I pointed out that it is important for dying persons to know that life is going on around them. I added that her father would feel less guilty about monopolizing her time at the hospital if he knew she was having an enjoyable life of her own.

A few days later, Cecily called back and said that her father had taken the news of the family vacation in the best of spirits.

You won't make Cecily's initial mistake if you include in your will a heading "Good and Bad News." Although you won't be able to fill in this section unless you are actively involved in the dying process of a loved one, the notation will remind you to talk about your ongoing successes and failures. A person near death continues to love you and wants to help with your struggles. Don't lock him or her out.

THE ILLNESS

How much about the dying person's condition should you keep secret from him or her?

When someone is sick you may consider hiding the severity of the illness. You rationalize that this is a good way to protect someone you love from undue stress.

In many instances it is not wise to deceive a dying person about his or her condition. Victor learned this the hard way when the illness of his father, Don, was diagnosed as terminal.

The doctor told Victor that Don had only two months to live. What he didn't say was that he had also told Don about the prognosis. Victor decided not to discuss this bad news with his father when Don came to live with Victor and his family.

Instead of facing the dying process head-on, Victor placed his father in a back room of the house. He, his wife, and children tended to avoid Don and rarely talked about his illness.

One night, while I was working on the suicide crisis telephone line, Don called. He explained that he was so depressed he was thinking of taking his life. He said that he had looked forward to dying around the people he loved, but had found that they didn't want to be with him at this time.

I visited the family and during our conversation, Victor discovered the startling news that Don knew his prognosis. There was great relief of tension in the house. After I left, Don's special bed was moved into the living room and he soon became involved in the household's everyday activities. Three months later he died in peace. Victor wrote me about how he and his family treasured the time that they had spent with him at the end.

I hope this case history encourages you to make a note in your will that says: "Don't be overly secretive with a dying person about his or her physical condition. Do find out from the doctor what he or she already knows."

The fewer walls you allow anyone's sickness to build, the freer you will be about discussing the illness. This freedom will enable you to release emotions while the person is alive, so you will experience less guilt and stress when he or she is gone.

Devise and Bequeath

Was this section of your personal secrets will more difficult to prepare than the first? Have you written down fewer secrets?

You probably did have a little more trouble deciding what you would disclose to a dying loved one. There are two good reasons.

1. It is easier to think about yourself on the deathbed revealing secrets than to think about standing over someone special who is dying and sharing your hidden thoughts. In the first position you sense that you have a right to speak up, but in the second, you may not feel as confident.

2. Many of the secrets that you need to put in the will cannot be completely filled in until the dying process begins. For example, discussing the individual's changing physical condition or your ongoing good and bad news.

Still, you are more aware of what you would like to say, what you shouldn't discuss, and what must be expressed. This awareness is invaluable because you are thinking in a responsible and discriminating manner. You have also taken the mystery out of what to discuss with a dying person.

As you did in Section I of your will, make a list of the secrets you plan to reveal, place the names of the beneficiary or beneficiaries alongside the appropriate revelation, and include the way you want to tell the confidence: either face-to-face or in a letter.

With these final notations, you have written Section II and the first draft of your personal secrets will. Although you have completed the document, it will never really be finished.

Revisions

If you have prepared a last will and testament or set up a living trust with an attorney, you know that from time to time changes need to be made. In a will, this alteration is referred to as a codicil.

There are at least four reasons why you may want in the future to revise your personal secrets will.

1. You decide to reveal some of the confidences that you have included because circumstances have changed. Waiting until you or someone else is dying no longer seems appropriate.

2. You end a relationship with a person and find the secret irrelevant.

3. You discover that the hidden experience has stopped affecting your intimacy with a loved one.

4. You uncover a new secret that needs to be added.

Periodically, do reread and revise your will. It is wise to keep it as up to date as possible. None of us knows our destiny or the fate of those who are close to us.

ADMINISTERING YOUR PERSONAL SECRETS WILL

When the day arrives for you to read your will, you will need to turn to the appropriate section and consider three factors: the secrets, the best moment for revelation, and the disclosure process.

Reevaluating the Secrets

Although you had very good reasons for including a secret originally, you will want to reevaluate it before disclosure. Some time may have passed since you placed it in your will, and circumstances may have changed. Instead of creating the intimacy you desire, telling the secret now could cause problems.

Take each confidence you plan to reveal and judge it by these criteria:

- I have thought about how the person hearing my secret will react.
- I have considered the feelings of others who may be involved in my secret.
- I am not out for revenge.
- I am prepared to handle a possible rejection and the resulting lack of support that my revelation may cause.
- I sense that my disclosure will increase intimacy.
- I am not sharing the confidence solely to fulfill my own needs.

After reconsidering each secret that you want to reveal, you may find that one or more of them could create a conflict. If you are unsure about the possible repercussions, why not seek a second opinion from an uninvolved, nonjudgmental third party? The fresh insight could give you the necessary perspective to make your decision.

Should you decide that it is better to remain silent, don't feel guilty or upset. Remember, your will is designed to prevent problems and it is helping you do just that.

The Moment for Disclosure

Once you have determined which confidence(s) can be revealed you need merely to note the beneficiary or beneficiaries and the revelation technique (face-to-face or letter) that you have chosen. Then you are ready to find the appropriate time for the disclosure.

Generally, the more open and receptive you and the person hearing or reading the confidence are, the better the experience will be for both of you.

It is not wise to reveal a secret if you are or your loved one is in severe pain and cannot think clearly. And don't disclose the confidence when others are in the room unless they are directly involved in the secret.

If you are sending your secret in a letter, be sure the dying person receives it while he or she is physically able to understand what you have written. Or if you want a response before you die, you will have to send your note so that it arrives in time for the person to answer. Should you not wish a reply, simply leave the letter(s) with a friend and request a mailing after your death.

Timing your revelation is important, and you will need to monitor either your condition or the dying person's so that your last opportunity for disclosure is not missed.

Disclosing the Secret

When you have selected the secret, the beneficiary or beneficiaries, the technique, and the moment, you are ready to reveal your confidence. The revelation will be smoother if you consider these guidelines.

If you are choosing a face-to-face encounter:

- Describe why you want to share the confidence with the person and mention your general feelings surrounding the incident.
- Reveal the secret.
- Let the individual react.
- Follow up the person's comments with your own and discuss the emotions that you have uncovered.

If you are writing a letter:

- Describe why you want to share the confidence with the person and mention your general feelings surrounding the incident.
- Reveal the secret.
- Write about your emotional reactions after your disclosure.

Considering these suggestions before you reveal your secret will help you clarify your thinking and will enable you to be more focused when you are talking or writing.

Helping Each Other

With all your preparation, you may still find you are a bit anxious when the moment of face-to-face disclosure presents itself. That is natural, and it is the perfect time to ask for assistance from the person who is hearing the confidence. Doing this will create total involvement and make the experience a mutual one. In life you had the responsibility of being there for each other and smoothing over the difficult moments. This is also true during the dying process.

The Inevitable

Preparing a personal secrets will and revising it from time to time is not easy. The process reminds you of the inevitable, your death and that of your loved ones.

It will be easier in the future to write if you think of the dying process as an exploration of your life. It can be a very freeing experience and can enable you to say things that have always been difficult to discuss.

With your personal secrets will, you can begin to regard the deathbed as a place for sharing confidences and special intimacy where you can finally face your past and reduce the strain your secrets may have caused. Your disclosures can be done without harming anyone, and you will not have to worry about your nature being either too open or too closed.

I encourage you to continue revising your personal secrets will. I am sure it will bring you a rewarding experience similar to the one I read about recently.

In *New York* magazine (June 27, 1983), Craig Unger wrote a fascinating story of the heiress and ballet patron Rebekah Harkness. With capital once estimated at over $500 million, she had founded her own ballet company and provided the backing for some of the finest dancers and choreographers.

In May of 1982, she lay dying in Room 1409 at New York Hospital. Bobby Scevers, her longtime friend and one-time lover, sat by her side. He realized that she might not know how much he loved her and this was his last chance to tell her.

"I love you, Rebekah," he said.

She sat up in bed. "You do? I always thought you hated being with me because I was so old and horrible."

"That's not true," he replied. "It's always been an honor being with you."

Just then Edith, her daughter, walked in and saw them crying. She gave Bobby a Kleenex and tiptoed out of the room to leave them together at this touching moment.

PART FOUR

The Secret Savvy Primer

II

The Secret Savvy Primer

SINCE we began our journey, you have explored the many facets of secrecy and disclosure, uncovered how your past has influenced your too open or too closed nature, and learned skills to manage secrets in the present.

To ensure that your future dealings with secrecy and disclosure are positive and to facilitate your evolving balanced nature, I have prepared an easy reference guide. This "Secret Savvy Primer" will help you:

- discover whether your secrecy/disclosure decision will have a constructive or destructive effect,
- identify the safest and most responsive confidant,
- determine the best way to tell a secret,
- decide how to be a good friend to a person revealing a confidence.

Whenever you become involved with a secret, you can refer to this primer. The guide is divided into four sections. The first two — Should I Tell? and Should I Keep? — focus on the appropriate secrecy/disclosure decision. The next time you need to make a choice, you can evaluate your reason for the behavior you have in mind and on the basis of these sections, decide if it is in your best interest.

The third section, How to Tell a Secret, shows you the most comfortable and effective manner to handle a revelation.

The fourth section, How to Listen, will describe ways you can help a person reveal a secret so that the individual gains perspective and you can avoid possible intrigue or entrapment.

The more you use this primer, the more sharply you will hone your secrecy/disclosure skills. Eventually you will be such an expert that your response will be instinctive. When that happens, you will have succeeded in modifying your too open or closed approach to handling secrets and achieved your goal. You will have acquired a balanced nature, one that is synonymous with secret savvy and mental health.

SECTION I. SHOULD I TELL MY SECRET?

"You'll find out anyway."
"It's driving me crazy."
"I want to feel closer to you."
"I need your help."

If one of these phrases is on the tip of your tongue, you are probably getting ready to reveal a secret.

Stop. Before you make that decision, consider whether or not it is an appropriate one. Now is the time to determine if your reasoning makes sense by comparing it with the nine basic reasons why people reveal a secret.

Those reasons are:

- to get it off their chest,
- to feel connected,
- to be true to themselves,
- to achieve reciprocity,
- to prevent discovery,
- to spread the good word,
- to cry for help,
- to show they're in the know,
- to get revenge.

Some of these reasons can cause abuse by disclosure and stimulate negative side effects that could lead to a mental health crisis. Others can help you use disclosure to your advantage.

Since you feel ready to tell a secret, let's examine your reason against the backdrop of these nine so you will be able to find out if your decision is appropriate. If you don't like what you discover, I will give you some dos and don'ts to help you handle the situation.

1. To Get It Off My Chest

"I have to tell someone or I'll go crazy. I'll tell you because you're nobody I know."

Lately your secret has become an uncomfortable companion. You have found that hiding what happened has not made living with the experience any easier. Although you would like to discuss the incident, you are too embarrassed to talk about it with anyone you know. After some thought, you may decide to risk rejection of a loved one just to get the secret out in the open, or you may opt for confiding in a stranger to relieve the tension. A stranger may seem safer because you won't have to worry about being embarrassed, humiliated, or blackmailed with the person's reaction. You can just walk away.

Nancy, for example, took the opportunity of sharing her secret with me one afternoon. For all intents and purposes, I was a stranger to her even though she had heard my radio show several times.

"I can't stop adding and subtracting," Nancy told me. "Whenever I see numbers, I start calculating them. If I'm in a department store, I add the sales tags. Should I be in a bank, I get involved with every number in sight. Then I can't stop tabulating until I reach an even total.

"Numbers have always fascinated me, but one day, a year ago, after helping my daughter with her math assignment, I found I needed to continue solving the numerical problems in the workbook. I've been adding and subtracting compulsively ever since.

"I feel like I'm going crazy. I've tried to change, but I can't, and I'm afraid to say anything to anybody." After a moment's silence, Nancy asked, "Can you help me? This habit and keeping it a secret is driving me crazy."

After talking a little more with Nancy, I learned that a year and a half ago, her mother had died in an automobile accident and a good friend's home had caught fire and nearly burned to the ground. Those two events had left Nancy shaken and unsure of the future.

She realized that she couldn't predict what might happen to her or those she loved.

I suggested that her tabulating of numbers was an attempt on her part to bring order into her life and to feel more in control. I encouraged Nancy to seek professional help because she needed to understand how to live with the unknown.

A few months later, Nancy called back. She mentioned that a therapist was helping her. She added that discussing her secret with me had relieved her anxiety and made it easier to talk about her habit with the psychologist.

If your secret is driving you crazy and you can't tell anyone you know:

DO tell it to an uninvolved, nonjudgmental third party. Merely revealing it will release tension and may give you some insight into your behavior.

DON'T expect a stranger to react like a loved one in terms of helping you solve a problem or providing you with loving insight. True relief and understanding will come only when you share your secret with someone you love or a mental health professional. A revelation to a stranger usually brings just temporary relief from the tension of being cut off from everyone.

2. To Feel Connected

"If I tell you, I won't feel so alone."

You have just met someone who is very special or a group of people. You want to feel more accepted. After careful consideration, you decide that revealing some personal information could deepen the relationship.

You are making an appropriate decision if you use disclosure to feel connected. By sharing your experiences you will show your trust, and by receiving acceptance, you will feel loved.

Dick, for instance, found that when he allowed his friends to see him as he really was, he no longer felt isolated from them.

I met Dick at a large public relations party. He began to tell me how pressured he was at work. Some encouragement on my part elicited that he was a leader in the gay community and recently had been spearheading a gay rights bill, which was facing a great deal of opposition. He felt exhausted but didn't want to show his fatigue or frustrations. He thought they might disillusion his staff.

I suggested that Dick share his real feelings with his coworkers. Maybe they were feeling the same way but were unable to express this down side for fear of his disapproval.

When I saw Dick several months later, he sought me out in a crowd to thank me for my advice. He said that sharing his feelings had inspired increased loyalty from his staff and empathy from his friends. He now felt more like an integral part of the gay community.

If you want to feel connected:

DO tell a secret to people who are special in your life. The more open you are in an intimate relationship, the more likely it is that you will experience acceptance and trust.

DON'T reveal too much personal information to fair-weather friends or mere acquaintances. If you disclose private thoughts that are too personal, you may make the other person feel uncomfortable because she/he may feel pressured to reply in kind. Or you might find that the secret you have told has become common knowledge and is being used against you.

3. To Be True to Yourself

"If I tell you, I'll feel I'm being honest with myself about myself."

You have become increasingly aware that you have a secret hiding inside that indicates you have a real problem. You sense that the time has come to admit to someone else that you need help.

Wanting to be honest with yourself is a very constructive reason for revealing a secret. Your decision will enable you to get help and to rebuild intimacies that you may have lost.

Betty Ford and Elizabeth Taylor offer striking examples of how this kind of disclosure choice can work to your advantage. Both women spent decades guarding their secret drug and alcohol abuse. Denial to themselves preceded their cover-up to the world. Making their substance dependency public was part of the process of accepting themselves and their own addiction. By being open about their commitment to beat the problem, they strengthened their resolve to succeed. They were less likely to go back on their word.

In revealing the severity of their addictions, Betty Ford and Elizabeth Taylor became inspirations to others. In many ways, these two women are now role models for people who live lonely lives of hidden desperation.

If you want to be honest with yourself:

DO tell your secret to a person who will be nonjudgmental and who will help you find professional help.

DON'T reveal your secret and then do nothing about it. Dumping your emotional problem on others is self-serving and nonproductive.

4. To Achieve Reciprocity

"If I tell you, you will tell me about yourself, and maybe we can be friends."

You may have recently become involved in a relationship that you would like to strengthen. Perhaps you long for a deeper friendship or a more intimate sexual bond. Since you know little about each other, you've been thinking about revealing some personal information. You are hoping that your move will encourage the other person to share in kind and through mutual disclosure, you will build trust and love.

The desire to achieve reciprocity is one of the best reasons you can have for telling a secret. By disclosing private experiences, you indicate how much you value the other person. If that individual reciprocates, the two of you know that you have something special.

Bess and Sylvia used this type of disclosure without really realizing it. One morning, quite unexpectedly, Sylvia told Bess that she was having an affair. She added that she knew they had never shared anything that personal before but she just had to talk with someone, and she considered Bess a good friend.

As Sylvia poured out the particulars, Bess listened compassionately. Her affection for Sylvia grew because she believed that the confidence she was hearing indicated how much Sylvia trusted her and valued their friendship.

Bess helped Sylvia through her ordeal and back to her husband.

She never made any judgments. She even told Sylvia how she had almost strayed from her marriage on two occasions.

Both women found that this experience solidified their closeness and enabled them to discuss things on a more intimate level in the future.

If you want to achieve reciprocity:

DO tell a secret to deepen a relationship. If you have known the person for a short time, start by revealing information that is not highly intimate. If the individual does not reply in kind, you will not have left yourself in a defenseless position with someone knowing something terribly private about your life.

DON'T continue to share secrets if the other person doesn't reciprocate with similar kinds of information. It could mean that he or she is not ready for the level of intimacy you need. You might try to talk to the person about the lack of reciprocity, in hopes that a response will be forthcoming, or you may just conclude that you are not a good match.

5. To Prevent Discovery

"If I don't tell you, you will find out from someone else and then you will be mad at me."

Some time ago you may have hidden an experience from someone you love. Now you realize that your secret is in danger of being exposed. You don't want your friend, spouse, or lover to find out about it, but you are afraid discovery is inevitable. You have decided that it would be best to tell that person yourself. Although you hate to open up, you feel you have no alternative.

This reason for telling a secret is a positive one, but it puts you in a terribly difficult position. You must approach your disclosure with care or you may say things impulsively that you will regret later. Still, this reason can relieve the anxiety you are feeling and bring you closer to the person who is hearing your confidence.

Beverly was forced into sharing a secret and then discovered that the experience was not as shattering as she thought it would be.

Beverly was twenty-two years old, single, and alone when she became pregnant. She wanted the baby but she was afraid to tell her parents about the pregnancy. She felt they would be outraged.

As the months passed, Beverly decided she had no choice but to reveal her predicament. She was living with her mother and father and it was only a matter of time before they would notice.

After talking with me on the phone during my radio program and hearing some of the other listeners' suggestions, Beverly mustered the courage to confide in her parents. They were furious, but eventually their anger subsided. It was then that Beverly called me back and said that her mother's and father's excitement about having a grandchild had dissipated their rage. They were now very supportive of her impending motherhood.

If you fear discovery:

DO tell a secret to the person who will be exposed to the confidence sooner or later.

DON'T allow someone else to reveal your secret. That individual may not know the entire story, and you could be left in a difficult position as you try to set the record straight.

6. To Spread the Good Word

"If I tell you, you will tell me, and together we can change the world."

You may have been through a traumatic experience and decided to keep it a secret. You may have felt that society could never understand. Recently, however, you have been hearing that others have shared your experience and as a consequence they, like you, suffered because of it. You now decide to speak up. You band together with those other individuals and reveal your mutual secret in hopes that it will stimulate societal change.

Whenever you tell a secret to spread the good word and attempt to change the world for the better, you are using disclosure for a good reason. Your revelation can help others deal with a similar problem or perhaps prevent them from having to confront the same suffering.

The fight for abortion rights demonstrates how this kind of reason for disclosure can be an appropriate decision.

For years women went behind closed doors to have an abortion performed and then stayed behind closed doors standing guard over their choice. With women's liberation, the doors slowly began to open.

In her book *Outrageous Acts and Everyday Rebellions*, Gloria Steinem writes about having an abortion after graduating from college and about deciding to tell no one. While attending an abortion hearing in 1969 to research a magazine article, Ms. Steinem heard women testify about their illegal acts. She wrote in her book:

> I sat in a church basement listening to women stand before an audience and talk about desperately trying to find someone who would help them, enduring pre-abortion rapes from doctors, being asked to accept sterilization as the price of an abortion, and endangering their lives in an illegal, unsafe medical underground.

These confessions changed Ms. Steinem's perspective on her secret. She wrote:

> I was no longer learning intellectually what was wrong. I knew. If one in three or four adult women shares this experience why should each of us be made to feel criminal and alone? How much power would we ever have if we had no power over the fate of our bodies?

In 1972, Ms. Steinem, along with Judy Collins, Mary Cunningham, Lillian Hellman, Billie Jean King, and others, signed a proabortion petition asking women to join them in "a campaign for honesty and freedom." By doing this they each revealed their long-held secret and mobilized the movement to legalize abortion.

If you want to spread the good word:

DO tell a secret but realize that there may be negative ramifications for going public with essentially private information.

7. To Cry for Help

"If I tell you, maybe you will save me."

In the past few weeks you may have learned that a good friend of yours is in trouble. Or perhaps you are finding yourself trapped in destructive behavior. You are concerned about speaking up because either your friend swore you to secrecy or you are afraid of people's reactions if you reveal what you have been feeling. Still, after some thought, you think that disclosing what is going on might be the only way to solve the problem.

A cry for help is a good reason to tell a secret, although it is not wise to wait until the situation has become unbearable.

Here is Teddy's and Elena's story. Elena was very depressed. She had been in an automobile accident in which her best friend was killed. Although she was in no way responsible, Elena felt guilty. One night she told Teddy that she had been thinking about killing herself. When he suggested that she talk to someone about her feelings, she told him that it wasn't that serious and begged him not to tell anyone.

Several days later, Teddy noticed that Elena had begun skipping classes and was becoming reclusive. He agonized over what to do and finally decided to see the high school counselor. Mr. Bruce encouraged Teddy to get his friend to see a therapist.

A few days later, Elena was sitting in Mr. Bruce's office. Her "cry for help" had been heard by Teddy and, in turn, by Mr. Bruce. After months in counseling, she began to realize that her mourning for her friend had been complicated by the recent loss of a favorite grandmother whom she had stopped visiting in the nursing home shortly before she died. Understanding her guilt helped her resolve her feelings.

If you are crying for help:

DO tell a secret to receive the guidance and support you need. Find a person who will be able to give you insight into your behavior. It could be a good friend, your mate, or a lover. Or you may want to talk with a professional mental health expert or a clergyman.

8. To Show You Are in the Know

"If I tell you, I will feel more powerful."

You may have met someone recently and you feel it is important that he or she should defer to your position of power or influence. You know you have worked hard for what you have attained and you want others to respect you for it. You decide that now is the perfect time to use the information you have from being in the community or with the company for several years to show this upstart exactly how "in" you are.

Making this decision on a consistent basis causes abuse by disclosure. Telling a secret to show you are in the know oftentimes ends up showing how insecure you really are.

I saw this type of abuse by disclosure unfold while I was flying to the West Coast. I sat next to a man and woman who were traveling together, evidently for the first time, on business. He had been with the firm longer than she and after two drinks, he lowered his voice and said, "Can I trust you with something confidential?" She leaned over and replied, "Absolutely." He then related how he had seen their boss out on the town several nights in a row with the same striking blond, and she was not his wife.

"And that's not all," he continued. His business associate looked at him in amazement and replied, "You certainly know what is going on behind the scenes."

The man's immediate objective had been achieved. He was showing that he was more in the know than she and, therefore, more powerful.

I'm not so sure that this female executive would be so impressed if her associate continued to pump her full of racy stories about their boss. Why, she might begin to wonder, does he need to do this?

If you want to show you are in the know:

DON'T tell a secret to gain prestige. You could end up on a disclosure treadmill where everyone expects you to be forthcoming with information about others. You will soon find yourself in a perilous position, with the possibility of discovery and then censure.

9. To Get Revenge

"If I tell you, I can get back at you for hurting me."

You may have lost an argument a few weeks ago or you may have been taken advantage of by someone you know well. Since nobody likes to lose face, you may still be reeling from the experience. Perhaps you have thought about some retaliatory action but you just haven't found the thing that would truly upend the person who hurt you. After some consideration, you decide to reveal a secret, because if you tell what you know, the individual who hurt you will be put in his or her place.

It is never a good idea to take revenge by using secret information. It is a destructive act and, although you may feel victorious, your victory will be short-lived. Soon you will find yourself in a web of intrigue and being regarded as a most untrustworthy person.

Godfrey realized how problematic telling a secret for revenge can be when he told his parents about his brother's vacation.

It all began when they were children. Godfrey and Win were always rivals for everything, including their parents' affection. When they became adults, their competitiveness increased.

One summer Godfrey's and Win's relatives planned a family reunion. Both brothers were to attend, then Win changed his mind. He decided to extend his business trip in London instead. He told his brother about his plans and asked Godfrey to keep them from their parents. Win then called his mother and father, saying that he was ill and couldn't travel.

Godfrey waited for just the right moment during the family reunion and whispered the truth to his parents. They were terribly hurt, and Godfrey basked in their belief that he was the better son.

When Win heard about what had happened, he was furious. He began to distrust his brother more than ever. Ironically, his parents admitted to Win a few months later that they had never really felt a confidence was safe with Godfrey.

If you feel like taking revenge:

DON'T tell a secret to make yourself feel better. Your "victory" over the person who has upset you will be fleeting. You will soon find that your network of love and friendship is undermined through retroactive distrust.

Your Disclosure Decision

Have you compared your reason for telling a secret with the "basic nine"? Have you decided that your decision is inappropriate? Or have you determined that your method of disclosure would be better served by revealing your confidence to a different person from the one originally planned?

In general you are less likely to suffer abuse by disclosure if you avoid reasons 8, "To Show You Are in the Know," and 9, "To Get Revenge."

As you can see, most of these reasons for telling secrets are positive. When you use them with the dos and don'ts that I have suggested, you will enjoy the true benefits of disclosure.

SECTION II. SHOULD I KEEP MY SECRET?

"Everyone would laugh at me."

"I'd lose her love."

"His parents would be livid."

"I'd be ruined."

Thoughts like these may be racing through your head if you are thinking you would be better off keeping something a secret. A recent experience may have threatened your image and your need for control and separation. You are beginning to feel that unless you conceal what has happened someone will suffer terrible consequences.

Before you make a decision not to tell, I would encourage you to think twice. You may find that your reason for concealment is not well founded. If so, it could lead to a possible mental health crisis.

A practical way to judge whether or not your rationale is valid is to compare it with the six most common reasons why people decide to keep a secret.

Those reasons are:

- to avoid ridicule,
- to avoid rejection,
- to avoid emotional blackmail,
- to avoid being negated,
- to protect someone special,
- to test someone's love.

Some of these can stimulate negative side effects that can harm your emotional well-being. Others have the potential of providing privacy and increasing intimacy.

To determine if you are about to make an inappropriate secrecy decision, let's review the six reasons why people keep secrets.

1. To Avoid Ridicule

"If I tell you, you'll think I'm weird or crazy and maybe tell me so."

You may feel that you have developed a strange habit or have become involved in peculiar thoughts. Your fear of being ridiculed makes you feel that you should keep your behavior a secret.

Be careful if you are considering this reason for concealment. You are not the best judge of your own behavior. Without the proper perspective, which usually comes from an outsider, you could undermine your self-confidence or repress a potentially dangerous emotional problem.

Al, for example, began to think that his habit of dress meant that he had transvestite tendencies. His identity crisis was directly related to his secret — Al wore ladies' pantyhose.

Initially, Al's decision to try nylons was his girlfriend's idea. Margo felt the stockings would keep him warm when he worked in subzero temperatures repairing utility lines. Al discovered that Margo was right about the pantyhose's warmth, but that didn't stop him from feeling self-conscious about having them on underneath his jeans.

After trying long underwear and other alternatives, Al went back to nylons. When he called me for advice while I was on the radio, he explained that he felt his preference for the pantyhose indicated that he might be a transvestite, although he never received any sexual pleasure from them.

I assured Al that he was not a transvestite. I mentioned that so many men had discovered the same solution that a company was trying to market a line of nylons for males. Their biggest obstacle was men's fear that they wouldn't be 100 percent masculine if they purchased stockings instead of sweatsocks.

A few months later, I heard from Al again. He thanked me for my insight and admitted that he now could laugh at his fears. He also added that he was sorry he had been so secretive for so long.

If you feel your behavior is weird:

DON'T keep it a secret from everyone. Your habit could be perfectly harmless or it could indicate that you have a psychological problem. Concealment will lead to poor self-esteem, anxiety, and blocked emotional growth.

DO tell your secret to an uninvolved, nonjudgmental third party who will honor your confidentiality and give you the proper perspective on your behavior.

2. To Avoid Rejection

"If I tell you, you may not like me anymore."

You are at a point where you want to talk about a very personal aspect of your life with a close friend, spouse, or lover. After some thought, you reconsider because you fear the reaction. You are afraid that you may expose a side of yourself that will cause that person to reject you.

Before you use this reason for keeping a secret it would be wise to consider why you need to withhold information from someone you love and what repercussions your concealment may have.

Jane, for instance, never thought that being secretive about her abortion would harm her friendship with Susan. She was wrong.

Although both women prided themselves on sharing their most personal experiences, Jane decided it would be best if she kept her abortion a secret. She was afraid of her friend's reaction. She knew Susan did not approve of such an act except in life-threatening situations. She also recognized that Susan tended to idealize her as an intelligent woman who was careful when it came to men.

Soon Jane became so concerned about Susan's finding out that she began to make excuses for not seeing her. After a month, Susan sensed that something had come between them. She suggested that they have dinner and talk over what was going on with their friendship. After too many glasses of wine the truth tumbled out of Jane's mouth.

To Jane's amazement Susan was more upset about her friend's secretiveness than about the abortion. To both women's credit, they decided to examine why Jane had used secrecy. They uncovered her irrational fear of rejection and discussed how she could deal with it in the future.

If you feel your behavior could cause rejection:

DON'T keep it a secret from those you love. In general, the

closer the relationship the less likely it is that you will be rejected and the more likely that you will receive insight into your behavior.

DO ask yourself if you are unable to share a secret with someone close: how can I believe that this person really accepts and loves me if he or she doesn't know me?

DON'T reveal your most personal confidences to fair-weather friends or mere acquaintances. Your fear of rejection may be warranted and your need to keep a secret may be appropriate.

3. To Avoid Emotional Blackmail

"If I tell about you, you might tell about me and I could get hurt."

You may have shared many intimate secrets with someone who is special in your life. Lately you are finding that your relationship has problems. You suggest two alternatives: you could seek outside help or end the marriage or friendship.

Your mate, lover, or friend doesn't like either suggestion and threatens that if his or her secrets become known, even in a therapeutic situation, then yours will be exposed. Additionally, you are told, if you leave the relationship he or she will reveal many of your secrets to others.

If you decide that you cannot deal with having outsiders privy to such personal information, you may allow yourself to be emotionally blackmailed. This reason for concealment could trap you in an unsatisfying and destructive union.

Sue's and Daniel's case history shows how emotional blackmail was used to their disadvantage and how it caused daily anguish and pain.

From the moment they shared their first night together on their honeymoon, Sue and Daniel became involved in a secrecy pact. Both felt that if anyone knew their secret, they would be emotionally destroyed.

After seven years of marriage, they found that nothing had changed and their secret was the same — they had never had sex.

Daniel wanted to file for divorce but knew that was impossible because Sue had threatened that she would tell everyone why he was leaving her. She would say that he couldn't perform in bed.

Sue continued to blackmail her husband because she was afraid of what would happen to her if Daniel ended their marriage. She didn't know what she would say to her parents, how she would find another man, and if she could support herself as a single woman.

After a while, Sue and Daniel became so unhappy that they sought marriage counseling. During their sessions, they spoke about everything *but* Daniel's fear of sex. They kept their secret safe.

Encouraged to get to the root of the problem, they began to talk openly about their longstanding secrecy pact. At that point, we got down to dealing with their real problems: her inferiority complex and need for control and his lack of assertiveness. Once they stopped blaming each other for being trapped in the marriage and started working on their own difficulties, they began facing their fears.

Today they are still together. They have not as yet consummated their marriage, but at least they do not use emotional blackmail for control. They are working on building a stronger union.

If you fear emotional blackmail:

DON'T allow secretive behavior to menace the relationship. Reevaluate your bond. It may be a destructive one and your silence could be a trap.

DO seek professional help. Talk with a clergyman or therapist. Your secrets could give you insight into your behavior. Remember that your privacy will be honored.

4. To Avoid Being Negated

"If I tell you, you may not believe me."

You have experienced something that you would like to share with someone special. After some thought, you decide to keep the incident to yourself because in the past, when you talked about similar situations with your mother or father, you were not taken seriously. You believe your mate, lover, or friend will respond to you in the same way, and that unnerves you.

Your fear of being negated can lead to concealment. It can cause you to distance yourself from those you love and perpetuate your parents' control over you even though you are an adult.

A case in point was Meg's. Although she was a successful and articulate attorney, she had difficulty telling her boyfriend about her sexual needs. In therapy I began to understand why she was so uneasy talking about sexuality. Her mother had changed the subject whenever Meg mentioned sex. This was dramatically demonstrated after a traumatic incident that occurred when the family went to see a movie together.

Meg, aged seven, had gone with her parents to a matinee. When she found that her view of the screen was blocked, she moved one seat away from her father. Seconds later a man sat down in the empty seat. Before Meg realized what was happening, he had placed her hand in his. Then he put both their hands in his pocket and wrapped her fingers around something hard and erect.

The man's grip tightened and a series of thoughts raced through Meg's mind. Did her father know him and was this a friendly gesture? Was he a doctor hired confidentially by her parents to take her pulse and determine if she was suffering from a ghastly disease?

When his grasp didn't loosen, Meg froze. She couldn't understand why her father didn't notice anything. Finally, she summoned all her courage and cried in a shrill voice, "Daddy, can I have some money for candy?" The man laughed nervously, jerked forward at the waist, and ripped her hand from his pants. She seized the money her father held out for her and ran from the auditorium. Minutes later Meg returned. To her relief the man was gone. She quickly sat down right beside her father and to this day says she doesn't know how the film ended.

Once she was home, Meg told her mother about the incident. To Meg's surprise, her mother said nothing and soon left the room.

Meg recalled that her mother's negation of her led Meg to assume the episode had been her fault. To compensate for that guilt, she decided never to tell anyone about anything sexual if she had some reservations about how that person might respond. As a result, Meg found herself withdrawing in intimate relationships with members of the opposite sex.

Therapy helped Meg understand her fears. She learned that her mother's behavior was probably an indication of the woman's own anxiety about sexuality and that it had nothing to do with Meg. This realization helped Meg begin to trust people, brought her closer to her mother, and improved her sexual relationship with her boyfriend.

If you fear being negated:

DON'T keep something a secret. Your behavior could be preventing you from enjoying an enriching interpersonal connection.

DO reveal your secret to an individual within your circle whom you trust. Select a person who is not burdened by anxieties and who will listen with insight. The reaction will probably lessen your fear, improve your self-esteem, and begin to position your parents' response in a different light.

5. To Protect Someone Special

"If I tell you, it might hurt someone I love."

You have privileged information about a friend, your lover or spouse. Now you are being asked to break your promise of confidentiality and discuss what you know. You decide to keep your promise and not tell the secret.

Concealing information to protect another's privacy can be a noble act. It can increase the intimacy that you share with the person and, if the information you are withholding is not harmful to anyone, you can keep silent with a clear conscience.

The *New York Times* reported on April 10, 1984, that Evelyn Hertzog and Dorothy Lindsay felt they were justified in concealing some personal information about their friend and Evelyn's sister, Mary Ellen Bader. Mary Ellen had stashed away about forty-five thousand dollars. Mary Ellen felt that her children were after her money and that, having had her declared mentally incompetent, they planned to get it.

During the court proceedings, Mary Ellen testified that she was competent, didn't need her son as a guardian, and had received the money after her husband had died. When the county judge asked where she had put the cash, Mary Ellen refused to answer.

The judge could not cite Mary Ellen for contempt of court because of her legal status as a mental incompetent. So he called Evelyn and Dorothy to testify. They too declined to tell where the money was hidden. After begging the two grandmothers to reconsider their stand, the judge said he had no alternative but to find them in contempt of court and order them jailed. Evelyn and Dorothy kept their silence while they were in prison. When they were released more than four days later under five-hundred-dollar personal recognizance bonds ordered by a federal district judge, they continued to protect their friend. Mary Ellen said that the three of them were standing for "truth, justice," and what was "right."

If you wish to protect someone special:

DO keep a secret but be sure that the information you are concealing is not perpetrating negative behavior or harming another individual.

DON'T be secretive if your motivation is to buy a person's love. Your overwhelming need to offer him or her protection from others could be misguided and you could hide information that should be known.

6. To Test Someone's Love

"If I tell you, how will I know whether you love me? After all, love means you should be able to guess my secrets."

You have met a person who seems just right for you. Since you want to be certain, you consider concealing information about yourself in hopes that he or she will guess your special needs.

This reason for lack of disclosure is often used to try to revive the magical connection you once shared with your mother. There is a pull back to the time when you ruled supreme as an infant and were cuddled, fed, changed, rocked, and adored. Your needs were met almost automatically. You wish for that kind of treatment from your friend or potential lover.

Concealing facts about yourself can create unrealistic expectations of another person. You may lose a perfectly wonderful individual because he or she can't second-guess your needs.

Amy had purposefully withheld information about herself from men for years. It was one of the reasons why she was still single. No one had the instincts that she wanted.

One day Amy arrived for her therapy session flushed with excitement. She announced that she had met "Mr. Right." She quickly described how Miles had seen beyond her independent, solid-as-a-rock persona. He had turned to her at dinner and said, "I have a strong hunch that somewhere inside you there is a little girl who wants to be looked after. She is huddling right next to the grown-up woman sitting across from me."

In Amy's mind, Miles had passed the test. He truly understood her. When we talked about what had happened, Amy agreed that he may have just made a lucky guess and that to persist with her present secretive behavior would be childish. She concluded that it would be better to ask for her desires and see if they could be fulfilled, rather than to wait for them to be magically uncovered.

Amy's decision led to a more adult relationship with Miles. One year later they were married.

If you want to test a person's love:

DON'T keep secrets that challenge the individual's ability to prove that a unique connection exists. Expecting another to read your mind is naive, although wanting him or her to be sensitive is natural.

DO assess someone's intuitiveness by watching his or her instinctive manner toward you.

DO ask for what you need. Then you can see how the person responds and truly find out if your desires can be met to your satisfaction.

Your Secrecy Decision

How did your reason for keeping a secret stack up against the six we have just considered?

Did you find that you were thinking of being secretive because you fear ridicule, rejection, emotional blackmail, or being negated? After some thought, have you decided that your concerns may be invalid and that you should reveal your secret to deepen your interpersonal relationships and gain insight into your behavior?

Did you discover that concealing certain information could protect someone special from the scrutiny of the outside world? Have you evaluated the material that you would keep secret? Is it harmless or harmful information? What have you chosen to do? Will you hide the facts and insure the individual's privacy or will you tell what you know and refuse to sanction destructive behavior?

Did you learn that you may want to be secretive because you hope the new person in your life will second-guess you? Have you realized that keeping a secret for that reason could prevent you from having an adult relationship with the individual? Has that realization convinced you to tell him or her what you really enjoy and who you truly are?

If you have honestly evaluated your reasons for concealment and found them inappropriate, disclosure may be the solution.

SECTION III. HOW TO TELL A SECRET

Revealing a secret can be either a liberating or debilitating experience. It all depends on how it is done.

If you tell a secret in the right way you can deepen the intimacy you share with loved ones, gain insight into your behavior, relieve personal problems, or help others deal with a trauma.

If you mishandle disclosure you can find your secret being used against you, discover that your friends have misunderstood you, learn that your private life is now public, or see that your revelation has sparked a mental health crisis.

There is no reason to suffer the negative side effects of mistelling a secret. If you have had difficulties in the past, it is probably because you told personal information for an inappropriate reason, to the wrong person, and in a way that missed the mark.

Zack made all those mistakes. It happened when he confided in people he assumed would understand his predicament.

For seven years Zack's wife, Christa, had been institutionalized in a nursing home. When he realized that there was no hope for her recovery, Zack began dating. Eventually he met Judith and, after some time, they began to live together secretly.

Zack was proud of Judith and decided that he wanted her to be accepted as his lover. He also needed people to approve of their relationship. One day, Zack took Judith to the nursing home and introduced her to the staff. He asked the nurses and attendants to keep his affair a secret from his wife. He then mentioned that Judith would be accompanying him on all future visits.

The staff responded with silent rage. They liked Zack and felt he should have a life of his own since Christa rarely even recognized him anymore, but they also shared a special bond with his wife. They agreed among themselves that he had put them in an untenable position. They didn't want to lie to Christa, yet they felt they should honor Zack's secret.

Although no one voiced disapproval, everyone at the nursing home began to ignore Zack and Judith. Finally he asked one of the nurses why he was getting the cold shoulder. She replied bluntly, "You should keep your private life out of our business."

I met Zack when he called my radio program. He was terribly upset by the nurse's remark and wondered if it meant that loving Judith was wrong. I reasoned with him that although his relationship with Judith was really none of the nursing staff's business, it would have been wiser to confide in a close friend rather than several acquaintances. The staff didn't know Zack well, and to ask them to become involved in an intimate secrecy pact was probably inappropriate. I urged him to seek acceptance from those who truly cared about him and his future.

Zack understood what I was saying and decided to tell his brother about his affair. He admitted that he was apprehensive but felt that he could take the risk now that he understood the basic problem.

You may be like Zack after he spoke with me. You may be ready to reveal a secret but are a bit unnerved by the prospect.

To make certain that your revelation goes smoothly, I would like to suggest that you follow these five basic steps: (1) examine your reason; (2) select a confidant; (3) rehearse the disclosure; (4) tell your secret, and (5) evaluate the results.

These steps for telling will take the guesswork out of this aspect of the disclosure process.

1. Examine Your Reason

You have probably decided to reveal a secret for a very specific reason. Before you do anything else, you need to evaluate your motivation. The best way to do that is to ask yourself if you are about to become involved in constructive or destructive behavior.

Your reason to reveal is appropriate if it causes you to:

- enrich your interpersonal relationships by increasing intimacy,
- improve your emotional well-being by getting you to someone for professional advice or personal help,

- stimulate societal change by focusing on a universal problem.

Your reason to reveal is inappropriate if it causes you to:

- take revenge by hurting someone who has harmed you,
- consistently show you are in the know by gaining power with privileged information.

Should you find that you are being lured into disclosure for destructive purposes, it is best to stop now. You could find that your revelation will make you feel victorious, avenged, and powerful, but those sensations will be short-lived. You will soon be caught up in a situation where the negatives definitely outweigh the positives.

On the other hand, telling a secret to achieve intimacy, help, or change indicates that your reason is constructive and that you are ready to move toward your goal.

2. Select a Confidant

Once you have decided that your motivation to reveal is sound, you will want to choose a confidant. This person is an important part of the process because he or she will need to honor your privacy, help you tell your secret, give you perspective on what you concealed, provide insight into your behavior, and assist you in any problem solving that might need to be done following the revelation.

The type of confidant who will be best for you needs four characteristics. Your confidant should be:

- nonjudgmental: by being noncritical, the person will not react to you in a moralistic way or force personal values on you,
- uninvolved: by being unconnected with the secret, the individual will be able to offer you fresh insight,
- interested in your welfare: by caring about you, this person will be invested in your emotional well-being,
- trustworthy: by believing in confidentiality, this individual will regard your secret as privileged information.

Before you finalize your selection, you may want to ask yourself the following questions about the person whom you are considering:

1. What is his or her attitude toward keeping secrets? In the past has he or she honored the confidentiality of my secrets or other people's?
2. Do I know this person well enough to risk my secret? Has this individual proven to be a good friend in the past?
3. Is this person in a position either socially or professionally to hurt me by abusing the information that I am about to reveal?
4. Do I know intimate secrets about this person or am I about to reveal something that will leave me vulnerable because he or she knows more about me than I know about him or her?
5. Am I asking the person to help me beyond his or her ability?
6. Do I feel comfortable and safe with this individual?

After careful consideration, you may discover that the person you had chosen does not meet the criteria. You will then need to find someone else. At the same time remember that you can always talk to a minister, priest, rabbi, or mental health professional. Before you disclose your secret to a clergyman or therapist, you will want to find out how comfortable you feel with that person. Talk with others who have sought help from that professional and pay close attention to how much at ease you feel during your initial meeting.

3. Rehearse the Disclosure

Although you may have found the perfect confidant, you still could be feeling anxious about revealing your secret. This is natural and it's the reason I would suggest a "secret" rehearsal. A practice run can help you relieve your anxieties and gather your thoughts. Then when you share your confidence you will be less nervous and your story will be easier for your confidant to understand.

There are four rehearsal stages, with each one building on the next and letting you practice in a different way. Basically, you start by preparing the script, then playing the material in front of a mirror, going on to audition with a tape recorder, and, finally, trying it out with a stranger if necessary. The practice sessions will take little time and you will be pleased at how they prepare you for your "secret's opening."

PREPRODUCTION NEEDS

Before you start, you will want to find a private place where you will not be disturbed for a period of time. Your bedroom may be the most suitable area because you can close the door if there are others around. Or you may wish to wait until you are alone in your house or apartment.

Once you have found the appropriate rehearsal room, you will need to gather a pencil and paper, a mirror, and a tape recorder. When you have your props, your practice sessions can begin.

PREPARING THE SCRIPT

After you sit down and make yourself comfortable, take a pencil and paper and begin writing the story of your secret. Don't think about spelling, grammar, sentence structure, or the proper sequence of events. Just let your feelings pour onto the page. You may want to begin with comments about your emotional state at the moment. If so, that is fine because the more honest you are about your feelings, the easier it will be to release the tension inside.

As you continue to write, you will want to include the content of the secret, the people involved, the circumstances surrounding the incident, the reason you decided to hide what happened, and why you think it is a good idea to reveal it now.

Keep writing until you sense that you have said it all. Once you have reached that point, you are finished with this stage and will probably need to take a breather. As you do, notice how you are feeling. You may already feel less tense. This process has begun to desensitize you to your secret.

PLAYING TO A MIRROR

When you have completed your script, you can gather your pages and move over to a mirror. Start this practice stage by reading word-for-word what you have put down on paper. Then toss your script aside and begin telling your secret to the mirror as if it were your confidant. Pay attention to your gestures and facial expressions. They may be constricted at first but they will loosen up. This is another indication that your anxiety is lessening and that you are feeling more in control of the situation.

Continue to reveal the secret in different ways without a script. As you repeat this exercise, you may discover that you are adding new information. This is a good sign and shows that you are becoming more comfortable with your disclosure and are fine-tuning what you will eventually say to your confidant.

AUDITIONING WITH A TAPE

After you have spoken to your mirror awhile, you can turn to your audiocassette recorder and flip the switch. By moving around the room while you talk instead of holding the microphone, you will feel less like a radio announcer and you will be more apt to say whatever comes into your mind about the secret.

When you have said it all, you can play back your recording. Don't take notes the first time you listen. Hearing your secret aloud without any distractions will give you new insight and release even more tension.

Once you have heard your comments through, you can replay the tape and take notes. As you listen, consider if anything should be excluded or if something else could be included. Continue to rerecord your secret until you feel you are ready for a face-to-face confession.

TRYOUT WITH A STRANGER

Having written, talked, taped, and heard your story, you are probably ready to speak directly with your confidant. If you are, move on to Step 4: Tell Your Secret. Should you need more time and practice, you may want to try out your secret on a stranger.

Someone you don't know is a good person to select initially to hear your secret because he or she is uninvolved in the incident and usually nonjudgmental about your actions.

We all have chances to talk with strangers. You can either wait for the opportunity to present itself or force a brief encounter. If you commute to work, you could take a different train or bus and look for a potential prospect. Then again, you might go for a walk in the park and find a bench where someone who seems willing to talk is relaxing.

After speaking with the stranger about routine matters like the weather, you can steer the conversation toward the general subject matter of your secret and then slip directly into the story. You can either say it is your secret or someone else's. Choose whichever is more comfortable.

Don't be surprised if after your disclosure, the stranger doesn't react in a highly positive or negative way. Since this person is not emotionally connected with you, he or she will not know the relevance of the secret to you. Still, you will probably receive feedback and a new understanding about what you have hidden. The reaction could make you realize that your behavior is not unspeakable, and you would do well to talk with a person who could really help.

You are prepared now to tell your secret. You have finished your written and verbal disclosure rehearsal sessions.

4. Tell Your Secret

Since you have already chosen your confidant, it is time to contact that person, set up a meeting, and reveal your confidence.

THE CONTACT

When you talk initially with your prospective confidant, you will want to judge whether or not the person is interested in helping you. Find out by being honest and saying that you have a secret you would like to discuss in the strictest confidence. You can mention the general subject matter so the individual can decide if he or she feels comfortable hearing the secret and is capable of helping you.

If the person you have selected reacts in an uneasy way, you may need to choose another confidant. Should he or she respond in a positive manner, you can arrange for the meeting.

When you are finalizing your plans to get together, ask yourself these questions:

1. Will there be adequate time to disclose my secret?
2. Will there be enough privacy for the discussion?
3. Will my confidant be in a receptive mood?

If you can answer yes to these questions, you know that the atmosphere for your disclosure will be unrushed, personal, and private.

THE MEETING

When you sit down with your confidant, you will want to check that nothing has changed between you since your first conversation.

Initially you will need to talk about confidentiality and then reassess the time, the place, and your confidant's mood. If these factors meet with your satisfaction, you are ready for the "performance."

Other than a glass of wine or a beer, it is wise to leave alcohol out of the secret-sharing process. Your telling should be based on a sincere desire to disclose with all your wits about you.

As you reveal your secret, you will find that your rehearsal sessions serve you well. You will be telling your story in a succinct way without excess anxiety. Your composure will enable your confidant to listen carefully and ask meaningful questions.

After you have finished disclosing your secret, you may want to take a few moments to relax and let the tension and guilt fall away. If you feel like crying, go ahead. Should you need a hug, ask for or initiate one. Your confidant will probably want to support you in any possible way.

5. Evaluate the Results

When you are through with your disclosure account, you will have three reactions: you will feel differently, receive a specific response from your confidant, and decide if you need additional help.

Once you have told your secret you will probably experience a wonderful sense of peace. This is because your secrecy strain, with its negative side effects, is subsiding. You are becoming less anxious and feeling better about yourself.

Don't be surprised if the person hearing your revelation begins to act a little uneasy. If he or she is not a trained mental health professional, you can expect two kinds of human reactions:

1. The individual will help you understand your behavior by relating something personal. When you hear his or her story, you must realize that it is probably being told to you as privileged information. This mutual sharing may give you more insight into your own secret and deepen the reciprocal nature of your relationship.

2. The individual will listen carefully and offer advice. After he or she feels you have the problem under control, the person may change the subject or leave. You may not hear from your confidant for a while, but that doesn't mean that he or she doesn't want to see you again or that you made a mistake by confiding in him or her. Listening to an emotionally laden secret often causes a distancing reaction. In time your friendship will be back to normal.

You may think that telling your secret and receiving advice has ended your problems. You could be right, but, to be certain, you need to consider the content of your revelation.

If you hid self-destructive behavior (alcoholism, drug abuse) or if you suffered from negative acts (incest, child abuse), I would encourage you to speak further with a mental health professional. By opening up a past trauma with a friend, you do relieve some anxiety, but to truly deal with the problem, you will need to mobilize help from people who have more expertise.

THE DISCLOSURE EXPERIENCE

The steps to telling can help you reveal secrets so that your disclosure is a positive experience. Use them whenever you feel like sharing a confidence. The insights and tension relief they will bring will make every step you take worthwhile.

SECTION IV: HOW TO LISTEN TO A SECRET

What happened the last time you heard a secret? Did it make you uncomfortable? Was the person's demand for confidentiality a problem? Were you caught up in a web of intrigue?

Being someone's confidant does not have to be troublesome. If you know how to protect yourself and help the other person, you can find the experience very rewarding.

Unfortunately, many people do not understand the basics of being a confidant. Damon, for instance, had no idea about how to handle a friend's disclosure. His naiveté prompted bad advice and involvement in an ugly situation.

One day Damon's friend Vince said he needed to talk with him.

He mentioned that he felt terrible about something that he had done. Damon was sympathetic and encouraged Vince to reveal his secret.

Vince explained that he had forged a check recently to pay for a hospital bill. He said he had found the blank checks quite by chance and since he had run out of money, he used one to take care of his son's emergency room visit.

Damon advised Vince not to feel guilty and added that under the circumstances, Vince's solution seemed to make sense. Then the two men shook hands and each ordered a beer.

Several weeks later a policeman came to Damon's office and arrested him on suspicion of forgery. When Damon asked the officer what he was talking about, the cop replied that he should ask Vince who had named Damon as an accomplice after he had been arrested.

At the police station, Damon demanded to know why Vince had implicated him. His friend answered, "You told me that there are good reasons to forge checks. It's all your fault."

Fortunately, Damon found a lawyer who was able to protect him, and the charges were dropped, but not before Damon's name appeared in the newspaper as a forgery suspect. Although a story clearing his name followed, it took Damon many months to live down what had happened.

You may never have to face the kind of severe repercussion that Damon did after hearing a secret. Still, you could find yourself in a very difficult situation if you do not know how to be a confidant.

Damon could have avoided any negative side effects of disclosure if he had told his friend that forgery was a crime and that solving money problems with illegal checks was self-destructive. By suggesting that Vince see a credit counselor, Damon might have been able to save his friend from committing more illegal acts resulting from money mismanagement.

The next time you are asked to listen to someone's secret, you may want to consider the five steps of disclosure listening. They are: (1) meet the person; (2) establish the secret's content; (3) set the scene; (4) listen and react; and (5) evaluate the experience.

These steps can prevent you from making a mistake like Damon's because each one is designed to protect you and help the other person. As you both go through the disclosure process, you will know when to listen and how to respond. You will also be able to tell if the

situation is too demanding or likely to involve you in destructive behavior.

Being a confidant can be satisfying, but it all depends on how you
take the steps.

1. Meet the Person

When someone comes to you and asks to tell you a secret, your initial reaction will be based on how well you know the person.

If you are close friends or if it is a loved one, you will probably be
delighted to listen. Should the individual be an acquaintance, you
may be slightly hesitant, not knowing what you are getting into.

Before you agree to be a confidant, you will want to consider how
you feel about the person, what your relationship is like, and how
the individual has been behaving lately.

If you are mad at the person, feel uneasy around him or her, or
detect destructive behavior, you may not want to hear the secret. Go
with your instincts. You cannot be helpful if you are angry and you
can be hurt if you insist on trying to assist someone who is known to
cause problems.

In general, when you are approached to listen, think about the
person who is making the request.

DO be open to hearing a secret from someone special. Part of a
relationship is supporting those you love and listening to them in a
way others cannot.

DON'T agree to being a confidant if you regard the person as a
gossip, troublemaker, or a deviate. Also feel free to sidestep the situation if you feel you are not emotionally up to taking on that kind of
responsibility.

DO consider listening to an acquaintance who has the potential of
becoming a friend or who has helped you in a special way.

2. Establish the Secret's Content

Once you have decided that you are receptive to being a confidant,
you will need to find out about the general subject matter of the secret. That will help you decide whether or not you want to become
further involved.

By not asking specifically what the secret is about, you allow the person a sense of privacy. Later, if you decide not to listen, you will not have left the individual feeling vulnerable.

People's reasons for revealing secrets break down into three categories: help, love, and power. You can identify which one is being used by the "telling" opening phrase. The three respective phrases are: "I need your help," "There is something you should know about me," and "I know something you should know." In most instances these brief sentences give you a good idea as to the type of secret you will be hearing. Then you will be able to decide if you are becoming involved in the kind of confidence you can handle.

I NEED YOUR HELP

This person is concealing a problem that is causing emotional difficulty. The subject matter could revolve around an impending divorce, an embarrassing habit, a serious illness, unusual sexual activity, or an economic setback.

If a person prefaces the secret with this phrase:

DO listen to someone special who is in trouble and needs a kind ear.

DON'T become a confidant if the subject matter makes you feel uncomfortable. Suggest another person who might be more receptive.

THERE IS SOMETHING YOU SHOULD KNOW ABOUT ME

This individual wants to reveal a highly personal secret in hopes that you will accept him or her in a more intimate way and perhaps reply in kind. The disclosure could involve a former addiction, sexual liaison, criminal act, or physical dysfunction.

If a person prefaces the secret with this phrase:

DO listen if you want to deepen the relationship and if you do not feel threatened about sharing private information with this individual.

DON'T say you will listen to the secret if you don't want to forge a closer link. There is no reason to be forced into secret-reciprocity.

I KNOW SOMETHING YOU SHOULD KNOW

It may seem as though this person only wants to help by sharing some special information with you. This may be the case. Keep in mind, however, that he or she may also want to establish his or her superiority. The secret could concern something only a few people know about in the community or on the job, such as a boss's private life, your recent affair, or a friend's alcoholism.

If a person prefaces the secret with this phrase:

DO listen and learn, but keep in mind the person's motivation.

DON'T get too involved in a secret of malicious gossip. You can always change the subject by saying that you aren't interested in becoming a party to this kind of confidence.

Having listened carefully to how the person who wants you as a confidant has introduced you to his or her secret, you are now in a better position to decide if you wish to get more involved.

3. Set the Scene

When you decide to be a confidant, you get ready to participate in a very special process. To make sure that the experience is comfortable for you and the person making the disclosure, you will want to bring certain personal traits to the situation and create a special atmosphere.

CONFIDANT CHARACTERISTICS

It is important that you know about the traits that make a good confidant before you encourage the person to talk about the secret. Otherwise, you may not be able to offer the optimum level of understanding and support.

You will be an effective listener if you are:

- nonjudgmental: your task is to give the person insight and help rather than a lecture;
- trustworthy: your confidentiality is sacred and you know how important the privileged information you are hearing is to the other person;
- uninvolved: your impartiality stems from the fact that you are not directly connected in an emotional way with the individual's situation;
- concerned: your interest shows that you care about the person's emotional well-being.

If you have all the confidant characteristics, you may want to reassure the person that you know what is needed to make him or her comfortable. This will reinforce the person's decision of having chosen you and will make him or her feel more relaxed about the task ahead.

SPECIFIC ATMOSPHERE

Listening is easier if you can find a special place, have allotted enough time, and are emotionally receptive.

The disclosure process demands privacy. You will feel less tense and more focused if you select a quiet place. Interruptions can be disconcerting and disturbing to you both. You need to give your full attention to the person and any intrusions could increase tensions or stop the revelation all together.

Be sure you have allowed plenty of time to hear the confidence and to have a follow-up discussion. Don't assume that what needs to be said can be done in five minutes. You may want to set aside at least an hour.

The more receptive you are when the secret is being told, the more likely you are to be supportive and helpful. If you are feeling fatigued or emotionally harassed, you will not be a good listener. Postponing the meeting would be a better solution than being only "half there."

When you know that the atmosphere is right, the time required is available, and your receptivity is good, you are ready to hear the secret.

4. Listen and React

As the person begins to talk, you will naturally begin to feel apprehensive. Part of the anxiety you are sensing comes from the individual who is telling the secret. He or she is on the line, risking his or her personal reputation.

There are three ways that you will be able to lessen the tension of the moment and help the person with the disclosure. They involve three modes of listening: quiet, empathetic, and helpful.

QUIET LISTENING

Initially you may think that you have to carry on an animated conversation to get the other person to relax. You don't. Just let him or her talk. If you interrupt with personal stories, you may think you are helping, but you are not. You are actually disrupting his or her thoughts. Telling a secret takes courage and is fraught with tension. Don't add to the anxiety with small talk, jokes or private vignettes.

EMPATHETIC LISTENING

As the disclosure continues, the person may begin faltering. You can encourage him or her to open up with phrases that reflect the emotions the individual may be experiencing. Phrases like "It sounds like this is really upsetting you" or "You seem worried about this" show how understanding you are about the experience. They also create an empathetic bond. Since these comments are nonjudgmental, the person feels that you are supportive and is reassured that any fears he or she had are unfounded.

HELPFUL LISTENING

There will come a point where the story will seem to end. This would be a good time to ask thoughtful questions. The content of your questions can assure the person that you have been listening carefully as well as help him or her look at the aspects of the secret that may not have been addressed.

Don't press too hard in any one area. Although the person has opened up to you, he or she may want to keep certain facts private. If you find a line of questioning that seems to upset the individual, merely back off.

When you have heard the confidence and gathered the information you feel you need, you will want to take a few minutes to think. Your initial reaction may be to jump in and give advice. Don't. Take time to remember what was said and then ask yourself a question, "Does this person want advice or should I be only a listener?"

If you aren't clear as to the answer, you may want to ask the person directly. You may be told that just talking about it with another person was enough. If that is the case, realize that you have completed your task. The meeting is over. An exception to this guideline would be if you had been told some unsettling information that alerts you to a serious problem that the person has not as yet faced. In that case, you may have to speak up.

Should you feel that some advice is expected, you will want to react realistically, honestly, and reciprocally.

BE REALISTIC

Don't minimize or normalize a secret. If you are told of antisocial behavior, such as shoplifting, don't say, "Well, I guess everyone does it from time to time."

Discuss how frightening it is to lose control like that and risk getting caught. You need not be judgmental, just realistic. By placing the behavior in a clear light, you are helping the person understand the future consequences.

Explore whether the person should tell someone else about the secret. By revealing the confidence to a loved one, good friend, or business associate, the confider may improve a relationship and be better understood.

BE HONEST

If you are surprised by what you hear, be sure to express those feelings. Remember that your feedback is important. Your reaction will give the person perspective on the experience. If you cannot offer guidance, say so but suggest where the person may go for advice.

DO RECIPROCATE

Once you have reacted to the confider, you may wish to share a private experience of your own. You may want to let him or her know that you have been there too. As you open up, remember to ask for confidentiality.

Don't feel guilty if you don't want to reciprocate at this time. One revelation doesn't automatically require another.

When you both feel that you have said it all, you may find yourselves emotionally and physically drained. It may be hard to say good-bye. Neither person wants the other to feel rejected. Take the initiative, end the meeting, and promise to keep in touch. Talking for hours or days on end won't accomplish a lot. Each of you needs time alone to digest what has happened.

5. Evaluate the Experience

As the confidant, you will want to think over what has occurred. You could do that by bringing someone else into the picture, but doing so is usually tricky because you are dealing with privileged information.

The easiest way to evaluate the experience is to keep in contact with the other person. Initially, that may be difficult because often after revealing a secret, a person feels vulnerable. He or she knows you have private information that is shocking or embarrassing. In time, however, as the individual realizes that you will not be the cause of ridicule or rejection, he or she will contact you. Until then, you will have to be the one who reaches out with reassurance.

Ask how things are going. Don't avoid mentioning the secret revelation. If you feel the problem is getting worse, discuss your concern.

The truest way to judge your actions is to realize that being told a confidence is an enormous compliment. You should feel a terrific sense of pride at having been asked.

Finally, you can look at yourself and see how you fared during and after the process. If you did not become involved in destructive behavior, were challenged by the revelation, and deepened a relationship, you can say that the experience was a success.

FUTURE STEPS

Once you have heard a confidence with the help of the five steps of disclosure listening, you will look forward to hearing the secrets of friends and loved ones. You will not be afraid to veer away from confidences you don't want to hear. You will find that your value as a person will rise in your own eyes and the intimacy that you share with others will increase.

Afterword: One Final Secret

DEAR READER:

We have experienced a long journey together, one in which we have explored your secrecy/disclosure nature. We have talked about its origins, seen how it influenced your life, and considered ways to modify it.

If you participated fully in the process of secrecy/disclosure modification, you will be a different person now than when you began this book. You will find that your approach to handling secrets is becoming more balanced and that your total personality is taking on a new look.

You may not have been prepared for a personality change, but it has happened, and I wanted to reveal that secret to you before we part. You see, your secrecy/disclosure nature is so basic to your personality that you could not modify one without affecting the other.

Perhaps you have noticed that some of the people closest to you may have been looking at you in a strange way. Many will recognize your change for the better and even comment on the positive aspects. Others — and you have to be prepared for this — will feel uncomfortable with the different you. They may even pressure you into reverting to your previously too open or too closed nature. Just remember that they may have a stake in your "old" self. You can rest assured that you are on the right track. After all, you have carefully worked on changing yourself throughout this book.

Now that the journey is over, I must remind you that it is really just beginning. You will continue to add balance to your secrecy/disclosure nature, become more of a secret savvy pro, and improve your secrecy skills whenever you use the techniques that we have discussed. As you handle secrets appropriately you will reap the rewards of deeper relationships and a more fulfilling life.

GOOD LUCK.